Bible ites

*To Mom and Dad, who embody so many
virtues of the ancients, and who first introduced
me to heroes from holy pages. I love you.*

—D.B.

*To Brooke—for staying up late with me
to work on the book and then going to bed so
I could get back to work. I love you.*

—R.J.

Text © 2015 David Butler
Illustrations © 2015 Ryan Jeppesen

All rights reserved. No part of this book may be reproduced in any form or by any means without permission in writing from the publisher, Deseret Book Company, at permissions@deseretbook.com or P. O. Box 30178, Salt Lake City, Utah 84130. This work is not an official publication of The Church of Jesus Christ of Latter-day Saints. The views expressed herein are the responsibility of the author and do not necessarily represent the position of the Church or of Deseret Book Company.

DESERET BOOK is a registered trademark of Deseret Book Company.

Visit us at DeseretBook.com

Library of Congress Cataloging-in-Publication Data

Butler, David (Seminary teacher), author.
  Bible ites : an illustrated guide to the people in the Holy Bible / David Butler ; illustrated by Ryan Jeppesen.
     pages cm
  Includes bibliographical references.
  ISBN 978-1-62972-108-8 (hardbound : alk. paper)
  1. Bible—Biography—Juvenile literature. 2. Christian biography. I. Jeppesen, Ryan, illustrator. II. Title.
  BS571.B88 2015
  220.9'2—dc23   2015018797

Printed in China   6/2015
RR Donnelley, Shenzhen, China

10   9   8   7   6   5   4   3   2   1

Bible ites

an illustrated guide
to the people in the Holy Bible

Written by David Butler

Illustrated by Ryan Jeppesen

Meet the Bible ites

Bible Time Line 2	Ruth 38	Peter 74
Adam & Eve 4	Samuel 40	The Woman at the Well 76
Noah 6	King Saul 42	The One Leper 78
Abraham & Sarah 8	King David 44	The Widow Who Gave Two Mites . 80
Lot & His Wife 10	King Solomon 46	Mary & Martha 82
Isaac 12	King Jehoshaphat 48	Pharisees & Sadducees 84
Rebekah 14	Elijah 50	Judas Iscariot 86
Jacob (Israel) 16	The Widow of Zarephath 52	Thomas 88
Esau 18	Elisha 54	Mary Magdalene 90
Joseph 20	Naaman 56	Pontius Pilate 92
Moses 22	Jonah 58	John the Apostle 94
Pharaoh 24	Daniel 60	Ananias and Sapphira 96
Joshua & Caleb 26	Shadrach, Meshach, Abed-nego 62	Paul (Saul) 98
Balaam & the Donkey 28	Esther, Queen of Persia 64	Philip 100
Rahab 30	Job 66	King Agrippa II 102
Deborah 32	Mary & Joseph 68	Lydia, the Seller of Purple 104
Gideon 34	Zacharias & Elisabeth 70	Jesus Christ 106
Samson 36	John the Baptist 72	

Even though the people of the Bible lived thousands of years ago, their examples and legacy are as potent and powerful now as they were in the past. Some of the people were faithful followers of God. They were obedient through difficult times and were witnesses of His miracles. Others chose to align themselves with wickedness, and they experienced great misery. The stories and people of the Bible span a time period of over 4,000 years and are varied and unique. Some of them were part of God's chosen people known as Israelites. Others were from neighboring nations and were called Canaanites, Hittites, or Amorites. With all of the variety, however, there is at least one thing in common among these "ites," or people, from the Bible: the lessons from their stories, whether good or bad, are lessons that can help you and your family in the decisions and challenges that you face today.

Have you ever imagined what the people of the Bible were like? Have you ever wondered why they lived the way that they did? What if you applied their stories in your own life? Maybe you can.

Bible Time Line

Birth of John the Baptist.

About 0 AD

Birth of Jesus.

Mary, Joseph, and Jesus flee to Egypt to escape the wrath of King Herod.

Book of Genesis

Adam & Eve

After the creation of day and night, land and water, and plants and animals, God created Adam and Eve, the first two people to live on the earth. Adam and Eve lived in a beautiful place called the Garden of Eden. While they lived there, they walked and talked with God. He gave them two commandments. The first was to start a family, and the second was to not eat the fruit from the tree of knowledge of good and evil. Satan tempted them to eat the fruit and transgress, or break the second commandment. When Adam and Eve did eat the fruit, they had to leave the Garden of Eden and could never return. They were then able to start a family and became the ancestors of every person to ever live on the earth.

 Adam was created first, followed by Eve. Eve's name means "the mother of all living."

 The event of Adam and Eve eating the fruit and having to leave the Garden of Eden is called "the Fall of Adam" or just "the Fall."

 Adam and Eve had many children and lived a long and productive life. Adam lived to be 930 years old!

 "So God created man in his own image, in the image of God created he him; male and female created he them" (Genesis 1:27).

Ashamed (Genesis 3)

One of the commandments God gave to Adam and Eve was to not eat the fruit from the tree of knowledge of good and evil. Satan tempted them, persuading them to eat it, and they did. After they ate the fruit, they could hear the voice of the Lord, who was coming to visit them in the garden. Adam and Eve were both ashamed that they had broken God's commandment by eating the fruit, so they hid from the Lord behind some trees.

"And the Lord God called unto Adam, and said unto him, Where art thou?" (Genesis 3:9)

Even though the Lord knew where they were, He still called through the trees asking Adam to come and talk to Him. Adam and Eve hid because they thought the Lord would be mad at them and punish them. The Lord was looking for them because He knew He could help them learn and progress.

Sometimes when we do something wrong, we try to hide from the Lord, our parents, and other people. Everyone makes mistakes and might feel ashamed, but we do not need to run from the people who love us and can help us face our mistakes and change for the better.

? Will you turn to God and those who love you when you have made a mistake and need help fixing it? Will you be honest with others about the help you need?

Activity

Play a few rounds of hide-and-seek. In the last round, give each person a treat when you find him or her. Explain that even though parents expect their children to obey the rules, there is no need for children to hide if they make mistakes—their parents will always love them and want to help.

Book of Genesis

Noah

 Many years after Adam and Eve left the Garden of Eden the world became very wicked. Noah, the prophet, was called to preach repentance and ask the people to believe in the Lord again, but nobody listened to him. The people were so bad that the Lord told Noah He was going to cleanse the earth with a flood. The Lord commanded Noah to build an ark, or a large boat, to save the lives of anyone who would listen. He also commanded Noah to gather the animals into the ark. Only eight people—Noah, his wife, their three sons, and the sons' wives—believed him and went into the ark. The rains poured down for forty days and forty nights, but the floods lasted so long that Noah and his family lived on the ark for about a year. When the flood was over, the Lord made a promise to Noah that He would never flood the whole earth again. Noah lived for 350 more years after the flood and was a righteous father, grandfather, and prophet.

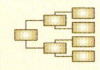 Noah was the great-great-great-great-great-great-great-grandson (that is seven greats!) of Adam and Eve. He was the great-grandson of Enoch, who with his people was taken up to live with the Lord.

 Noah preached and warned the people for over 100 years before the flood ever came.

 The Bible says the ark was three stories high and 300 cubits long by 50 cubits wide. Many modern scholars believe that is about 100,000 square feet (which is bigger than twenty standard basketball courts).

 Noah was born around the year 2944 BC and died around 1994 BC at the age of 950 years.

 "By faith Noah, being warned of God of things not seen as yet, moved with fear, prepared an ark to the saving of his house . . . and became heir of the righteousness which is by faith" (Hebrews 11:7).

Thus Did Noah (Genesis 6–9)

Noah was born and lived in the world during an extremely wicked time. Many later prophets and writers in the Bible used the time of Noah as an example of great unrighteousness among the people. Because of Noah's goodness, he found grace in the eyes of the Lord and was commanded to do many difficult things. Noah preached to people who ignored and hated him for over 100 years. Later, he was commanded to build a giant ark, following very specific instructions. After the ark was finished, Noah had to gather at least two of every animal that God commanded him to gather (for some animals, he was commanded to gather seven!). Then he and his family had to live with the animals on the ark for about a year. When Noah's family got off the ark, they had to start over, living all alone in the great big world.

"Thus did Noah; according to all that God commanded him, so did he." (Genesis 6:22)

Every time the Lord asked Noah to do something, he did it—no matter what it was. Sometimes the Lord might ask us to do big things. He might ask us to do hard things. We can respond the same way Noah did and do all that the Lord asks us to do.

? Will you do all that the Lord asks you to do—no matter what He asks?

Activity

Discuss stories of your own ancestors or others from the scriptures who did extraordinary things to be faithful to God. You may need to research some of these stories ahead of time.

Book of Genesis

Abraham & Sarah

Abraham and Sarah are two of the most recognized people from the Bible. They are studied and loved by many people—including people of other religions. Abraham and Sarah lived the beginning of their lives in the land of Ur. God commanded them to leave that land and the false religion of their fathers. Abraham and Sarah's original names were Abram and Sarai. The Lord changed their names when they made great covenants with Him. The Lord promised Abraham and Sarah that they would be the parents of a vast posterity that would number as many as the stars. They had to wait a long time for this promise to be fulfilled and did not have a child until they were very old. They were also promised that they would inherit a promised land called Canaan and that their family would bless all the other nations of the earth. This faithful couple passed through many trials in their lives, but they never wavered from trusting in God's promises.

 Abraham's name means "father of many," and Sarah's name means "lady, princess, noblewoman."

 Isaac, the promised son of Abraham and Sarah, was born when Abraham was 100 and Sarah was 90.

 Abraham and Sarah were promised that the Savior would be born through their family line.

 "And I will establish my covenant between me and thee and thy seed after thee in their generations for an everlasting covenant, to be a God unto thee, and to thy seed after thee" (Genesis 17:7).

People, Not Things (Genesis 12)

From the time he left Ur, Abraham's nephew Lot traveled with them. Abraham became very rich in cattle, silver, and gold. As his herds of cattle increased, it became difficult for Abraham's and Lot's cattle to share the land. The herdsmen began to fight with each other over the land and the grass for their cattle to eat. This fight could have caused a fight and division between Abraham and Lot as well. Abraham did not want this, and he came to Lot with a peaceful solution.

"Is not the whole land before thee? separate thyself, I pray thee, from me: if thou wilt take the left hand, then I will go to the right; or if thou depart to the right hand, then I will go to the left." (Genesis 13:9)

Lot looked both directions and decided to take the land that looked like it had the most water and best plants. Abraham happily took the land in the other direction—the worse choice—without any complaint. To Abraham, his relationship with his nephew mattered more than having better land for his cattle and the chance to be richer.

There are times when we fight and lose relationships and friendships because we argue over earthly things. It is easy to forget that people are more important than things. We can take Abraham's approach as the peacemaker and make sacrifices in order to show love to others. Having nice things is never more important than being good to people.

? Will you make choices in your life that show that people are more important to you than things?

Activity

Brainstorm a list of ways your family members can use their favorite possessions to help make somebody else happy. Throughout the week, report back to each other about the experiences you have acting on these ideas.

Lot & His Wife

Book of Genesis

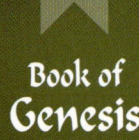

Lot was a faithful man with a tragic story. He lived with Abraham, his uncle, in the land of Ur before the Lord commanded Abraham to leave. Lot traveled with Abraham to Haran and then to Canaan, to Egypt, and back to Canaan. When the two of them split from each other, Lot chose to go to the fertile plains of Jordan. The land was wonderful, but it was close to the cities of Sodom and Gomorrah. Unfortunately, the wickedness of those cities had a negative influence on Lot and his family. On one occasion, Lot was captured by neighboring kings in a battle against Sodom. Abraham and his servants rescued him, and Lot moved back to Sodom. Eventually, because of his foolish choices, Lot lost most of his family in the destruction of Sodom and Gomorrah.

 Lot's father was Abraham's brother, Haran. When Haran died, Lot stayed with his uncle, Abraham, and his grandfather, Terah.

 The descendants of Lot are the Moabites and Ammonites, who became enemies to the Israelites (descendants of Abraham, Isaac, and Jacob) throughout their history.

 The Savior told the story of Lot and his wife to the Pharisees when He taught them about His Second Coming (see Luke 17).

 Scholars believe the cities of Sodom and Gomorrah were near the Dead Sea.

 "Remember Lot's wife" (Luke 17:32).

What You Face, You Embrace (Genesis 19)

When Abraham's and Lot's herds of cattle got too large and they needed to part ways, Abraham gave Lot the first choice of land. Lot chose the land that was more fertile and had more water. Unfortunately, it was also near the wicked cities of Sodom and Gomorrah.

"Lot dwelled in the cities of the plain, and pitched his tent toward Sodom." (Genesis 13:12)

Even though he wasn't living in Sodom, Lot lived nearby and faced his tents toward the wicked city. Before long, Lot and his family moved into the city. One day, God sent messengers to Sodom to warn Lot that the cities would be destroyed due to the people's wickedness, but Lot ignored their warnings. Eventually, the messengers were more forceful and brought Lot, his daughters, and his wife out of the city. His two sons-in-law did not believe him and were in the city when fire and brimstone rained down on it. Even though she was warned not to, Lot's wife looked back at Sodom and was turned to a pillar of salt. Lot lost what was dear to him in a series of events that all started by simply pitching his tents toward Sodom.

What we face in life, we eventually embrace. Most tragic stories start with just a hint of danger. The smallest amount of evil can grow rapidly until it is too late.

? Will you get rid of anything in your life that is even a little bit evil? Will you turn your back fully to wickedness and not have anything to do with it?

Activity

Prepare a beautiful ice cream sundae or other treat. Ask your family members if they want to eat it. Before they dig in, tell them you have one more ingredient to add. Add mustard, a pickle, or even a bug! Talk about how just as one small thing can ruin the whole dessert, even a little bit of evil in our lives can spoil us. Then enjoy a real treat together!

Book of Genesis
Isaac

 Isaac is the miracle son and only child of Abraham and Sarah. The Lord promised Abraham and Sarah that they would be the heads of a large family line. Isaac was the fulfillment of that prophecy, but he was not born until his parents were very old. The Lord later tested Abraham by asking him to sacrifice Isaac, his beloved son. All of the promises of land and a great family that the Lord made to Abraham were also promised to Isaac. When he was older, Isaac married a faithful and wonderful wife named Rebekah. Isaac and Rebekah could not have children easily, but eventually they were blessed with twins, Jacob and Esau. Isaac and Rebekah were faithful to the Lord their whole lives.

 Isaac's name means "he laughs." This could likely be a reference to Abraham and Sarah's reaction when they learned they would have him in their old age. It was probably laughter of shock and joy.

 We do not know how old Isaac was when the Lord commanded Abraham to sacrifice him, but many scholars believe he was at least a teenager or young adult.

 The Lord commanded Abraham to sacrifice Isaac at a place called Moriah. The traditional site known as Mount Moriah is in present-day Jerusalem, near the place called the Temple Mount.

 Isaac lived in the promised land of Canaan most of his life.

 "Sojourn in this land, and I will be with thee, and will bless thee; for unto thee, and unto thy seed, I will give . . . and I will perform the oath which I sware unto Abraham thy father" (Genesis 26:3).

Thine Only Son (Genesis 22)

Abraham and Sarah prayed and pled with God for many, many years before He blessed them with a son. God tested their patience, trust, and faith in Him. It was a miracle and a cause for celebration when Isaac was born. Can you imagine the feeling in Abraham's heart years later when the Lord commanded him to take Isaac on a journey to a mountaintop to be sacrificed? Can you imagine how Isaac felt? The journey was three days long, and every step must have been difficult. Isaac carried the wood on his back up to the place that God had commanded. Even though Isaac could most likely have overpowered his father, he allowed Abraham to tie him to the altar. He humbly submitted to God's command. Right when the knife was raised in the air, a heavenly messenger appeared and stopped Abraham.

"Because thou hast done this thing, and hast not withheld thy son, thine only son: That in blessing I will bless thee, and in multiplying I will multiply." (Genesis 22:16–17)

God blessed Abraham and Isaac and their posterity with unimaginable blessings because of their obedience to this test of faith. Many people compare this moment to the gift of God offering His Son, His only Son, for the sins of the world. Isaac humbly submitted like the Savior.

? Is there anything you would withhold from the Lord? Will you live your life as an offering to the Lord in thanksgiving for when He offered everything for you?

Activity

Make a list of as many things you can think of that God has offered to you and your family in your lifetime. Ask each person to decide one thing they will do this week as an offering of thanksgiving in return.

Rebekah
Book of Genesis

Although the history books and Sunday discussions usually speak of the faith of Abraham, Isaac, and Jacob, it is very important to remember the righteous and powerful women of the Bible as well. Rebekah was the wife of the prophet Isaac and the mother of the prophet Jacob. Abraham, Rebekah's father-in-law, sent his servant many miles from his home to find a wife for his son, Isaac. Abraham made his servant promise he would find a wife who was obedient to God and His covenants. The servant found Rebekah, who trusted in the Lord and left her own home to marry Isaac, whom she had never met. Rebekah, like her mother-in-law, Sarah, and her daughter-in-law, Rachel, had a difficult time having children. The only children she had were Jacob and Esau, who were twins.

 Rebekah had righteous desires for her family and hoped her sons would marry women who loved the Lord. When Esau didn't, she was full of sorrow.

 Rebekah guided Jacob, her younger son, into receiving the responsibility to lead the family when Isaac died.

 Rebekah was a distant relative of Abraham. That is why Abraham knew where to send his servant.

 Isaac and Rebekah are the grandparents of the twelve sons of Jacob, who later became the heads of the Twelve Tribes of Israel.

 "And they blessed Rebekah, and said unto her, Thou art our sister, be thou the mother of thousands of millions" (Genesis 24:60).

The Camels, Too! (Genesis 24)

Eliezer, the servant of Abraham, was given a crucially important mission when his master sent him to find a wife for his miracle son, Isaac. After a long and difficult journey, the servant of Abraham knelt down outside the walls of the city and offered a prayer. He prayed that he would be given a sign to know the right woman for his master's son. He asked that the woman appointed to be Isaac's wife would offer him a drink of water and then offer to give all of his camels a drink as well. Sure enough, when the women came to the well, Rebekah offered to draw him water from the well. She did it with quick compassion. Immediately after, to the servant's delight, Rebekah offered more.

"I will draw water for thy camels also, until they have done drinking. And she hasted, . . . and ran again unto the well . . . and drew for all his camels." (Genesis 24:19–20)

And so he waited until she had given drink after drink to all ten camels.

When every camel had its fill, Rebekah offered the servant a place to stay, boarding for his camels, and a hot meal before bed. Eliezer knew he had found the right woman for Isaac.

Rebekah saw a stranger and not only offered to serve him but went above and beyond common courtesy. She gave much and then more. It was a reflection of her heart.

? Will you offer your hand and heart to those around you? When you serve, will you serve more than is expected?

Activity

Make a family service jar. Have everyone write down something they would enjoy someone doing for them, put their name on it, and put it in a jar. Throughout the week, anyone else can draw out a random slip of paper and perform that act of service. Try to go above and beyond what is expected.

Jacob (Israel)

Book of Genesis

For many years, Isaac and Rebekah were unable to have children, which made them very sad. Isaac prayed to the Lord, asking for Rebekah to bear a child, and the Lord answered the prayer with twins. Jacob was the younger twin but eventually gained the family birthright and led the family in place of his twin brother, Esau. The Lord changed Jacob's name to Israel, and his descendants were known by this name throughout history—Israelites. Jacob was the father of twelve sons, whose descendants are called the Twelve Tribes of Israel. Descendants of these sons identified themselves by their "tribe," or family line, throughout the Bible. Jesus Christ, for example, is from the tribe of Judah, who was one of the twelve sons of Jacob. Jacob's family lived most of their life in Canaan, the promised land given to their family, but they moved to Egypt at the end of his life.

 The birthright blessing was usually given to the oldest son. It was a privilege and a great responsibility to lead the family spiritually and financially.

 The sons of Jacob were Reuben, Simeon, Levi, Judah, Zebulon, Issachar, Dan, Gad, Asher, Naphtali, Joseph, and Benjamin.

 Jacob worked for fourteen years for his father-in-law in order to be able to marry Rachel. The scriptures say it felt like a few days to him because of how much he loved her. She died delivering Benjamin, their youngest son.

 Thy name shall be called no more Jacob, but Israel: for as a prince hast thou power with God and with men, and hast prevailed" (Genesis 32:28).

To Always Remember (Genesis 28)

As Jacob grew older and it was time for him to marry, his father, Isaac, sent him off on a journey to find a faithful woman. One night, when he stopped to sleep, he gathered stones and piled them up as pillows for his bed. As he slept, he had a most magnificent dream. He saw a ladder that stretched from the highest part of heaven all the way down to the earth. Beautiful angels were going up and down the ladder. He saw the Lord standing above the ladder in all His glory. The Lord called to Jacob and promised him all the wonderful blessings that He had promised to his father, Isaac, and grandfather, Abraham. The Lord also comforted Jacob and said that He would be with him in life wherever he went.

"And Jacob awaked out of his sleep, and he said, Surely the Lord is in this place; and I knew it not." (Genesis 28:16)

Jacob woke up early and set the stones he used as pillows into a pillar, marking that spot as a special place. He named the area Beth-el, which means "House of God." He kept his pillar of stones there as a reminder of the glory of God and the special experience he had there.

We all have special spiritual experiences in our lives when God reaches out to us and we know He is there. These are memories we should keep close and always remember.

? Will you recognize, record, and remember the times you feel God's love?

Activity

Our special experiences can be easy to forget. Have everyone write down a special spiritual memory or find an object that represents a time God has answered prayers or shown His love. Put these in a place where they will serve as a constant reminder of God's love.

Esau

Book of Genesis

 Esau and Jacob were the twin sons of Isaac and Rebekah and the grandsons of Abraham and Sarah. Esau was a skilled hunter and would often bring the meat he caught back home to his father, Isaac, who favored Esau over Jacob. When it was time for marriage, Esau married a woman who did not believe in God. This made his parents upset. Esau was the older of the twins and should have had the family birthright, but he forfeited it to his brother Jacob. After a hunting trip when Esau was very hungry, he sold his birthright to Jacob in exchange for a bowl of pottage. Later, he was extremely angry when their father gave Jacob the birthright blessing, and Esau plotted to kill his brother. The two brothers were in a long, angry fight, but after many years, Jacob and Esau met again and Esau forgave Jacob and the two brothers were reunited.

 The name Esau means "hairy" and was given to him because of the red hair on his body when he was born.

 The twin brothers struggled inside of Rebekah before they were born. She prayed about the meaning of it and the Lord told her that the brothers would head two nations and the older would serve the younger.

 Jacob was born holding onto the heel of Esau.

 Esau's descendants were called Edomites. The Edomites were conquered by the Israelites and served them during the time of King David and long after.

 "Two nations are in thy womb, and two manner of people shall be separated . . . and the one people shall be stronger than the other people; and the elder shall serve the younger" (Genesis 25:23).

A Mess of Pottage (Genesis 25)

The brothers Esau and Jacob were drastically different and cared about different things. Esau was a mighty hunter, and Jacob preferred to tend the flocks near his home.

One day, Esau came home from the fields tired and hungry. He had been out hunting and had not eaten for a long time. Jacob had been near the tents and had prepared a bowl of pottage to eat. When Esau saw and smelled the dinner, he begged Jacob for it. Jacob asked Esau to trade his birthright for the bowl of pottage. Esau seemed to think his responsibilities and birthright privilege were not very valuable.

"What profit shall this birthright do to me?" (Genesis 25:32)

In a moment when he was desperate for food, Esau sold his special birthright for a bowl of beans and soup. His stomach was full, but his future was empty.

There are many things that we may want in this life. There are things we may hunger for. There are also many special blessings that God has promised to us. We need to be careful to not trade the special blessings of tomorrow for the things we hunger for right now. Don't give up your heavenly blessings for earthly pottage.

? Will you control your decisions and choices now to be sure you are worthy to claim the blessings God wants to give you in the future?

Activity

Put a small treat in front of everyone (preferably before the lesson begins). Tell everyone they can have the small treat now or any time throughout the discussion, or they can wait for a bigger one at the end. At the end, give the bigger treat to those who waited, and talk about what this example teaches.

Book of Genesis
Joseph

Jacob (Israel) had twelve sons but seemed to favor his second youngest, Joseph. He gave him a colorful coat as a gift of his love, and Joseph wore it with great pride. His older brothers hated him and were jealous. Their bitterness worsened when Joseph had dreams of being a ruler over them. In anger, they sold him to a group of travelers heading to Egypt. They tore up his coat and dipped it in goat's blood to convince Jacob that Joseph had been killed by wild animals. Joseph spent many years as a slave in the house of Potiphar, the rich man who bought him, until Potiphar's wife accused Joseph of attacking her. He spent years in jail for a crime he did not commit but was eventually released by Pharaoh, the leader of Egypt, so Joseph could interpret his dreams. Pharaoh loved and trusted Joseph, and he became the second in command in Egypt. As a ruler, he helped the Egyptians save food for a time of famine. Eventually, his brothers, who were starving from the famine, came to Egypt for food. They did not recognize Joseph at first, but Joseph forgave them for what they had done. Then his whole family, including his elderly father, Jacob, moved to Egypt.

 Joseph was the great-grandson of Abraham and Sarah and the grandson of Isaac and Rebekah.

 Joseph was seventeen years old when his brothers sold him to slave traders. He was thirty when he became second in command in Egypt.

 Joseph organized the effort of saving food in Egypt for seven years in preparation for the seven years of famine the Lord told him was coming.

 Joseph's Egyptian name was Zaphnath-paaneah. He married an Egyptian woman named Asenath and had two sons, Ephraim and Manasseh.

 "And Pharaoh said unto his servants, Can we find such a one as this is, a man in whom the Spirit of God is?" (Genesis 41:38).

God Makes It Good (Genesis 37–45)

Can you imagine how Joseph felt lying in the bottom of a pit where his brothers had thrown him? Can you imagine how he felt as he rode off in captivity to a faraway country to be a slave? Joseph's life seemed like it was headed for disaster. But God made it good, and even as a slave he became the most trusted of all his master's servants. Hard times came again when his master's wife lied about him and caused him to be sent to prison.

"But the Lord was with Joseph, and shewed him mercy." (Genesis 39:21)

God again made the experience good, and Joseph became the head prisoner and was able to bring peace to a fellow convict. He was forgotten in prison for a while, but God made it better by helping another person remember Joseph and his gifts. Eventually, Joseph became a ruler of Egypt—and just in time. He helped the Egyptians prepare before a great famine came to the land. Many families in the area were starving and running out of food—including Joseph's brothers and father, who still lived in the town where he grew up. They were starving and near death, but God made things good and arranged a deliverer for them in Egypt—their brother Joseph.

Sometimes bad things, unfair things, and hard things happen in life, but God can always make them become something good.

? Will you trust in the power God has to make something good? Will you respond to your trials and struggles with faith, hope, and trust in Him?

Activity

Get some play dough or molding clay for everyone. Have everyone turn their lump of clay into a fun sculpture. Explain how we are like clay in the Lord's hands. Even though some changes and experiences might hurt, He is molding us into something great. He can make us good.

Book of Exodus
Moses

 Moses was born during a terrible time in the history of his people. The Israelites were living as slaves in Egpyt. Pharaoh was nervous about there being too many Israelites, so he ordered every baby boy to be killed. Moses's mother saved his life by hiding him in a basket and slipping him into the reeds by the river. Pharaoh's daughter found Moses's basket and raised him as royalty in Egypt. We don't know when Moses found out he was an Israelite, but one day he killed a servant of the king to protect one of the Israelite slaves. He escaped Egypt and lived in a land called Midian for forty years. He got married and had children before God called him to return to Egypt to deliver the Israelites. After much persuasion and a miraculous escape, the Israelites wandered in the wilderness for forty years with Moses as their leader. During that time, Moses spoke with God on Mount Sinai and received the Ten Commandments, performed many miracles, and revealed the instructions to build the tabernacle, a portable temple. Although Moses wandered with the Israelites for forty years, he died before he entered the promised land.

 Moses was about forty years old when he ran away from his life in Egypt.

 The Lord appeared to Moses in the form of a burning bush to tell him to return to Egypt. Moses was about eighty years old at that time.

 Moses is mentioned by name in the Old Testament over 750 times. He is mentioned in the New Testament more than 75 times. He was loved and respected by many generations of believers.

 Moses was a descendant and a member of the tribe of Levi, one of Jacob's (Israel's) twelve sons.

 "Moses . . . choosing rather to suffer affliction with the people of God, than to enjoy the pleasures of sin for a season . . . he forsook Egypt" (Hebrews 11:24–25, 27).

Deliver Us! (Exodus 7–14)

After serving as slaves for over 400 years, the Israelites did not have the strength or endurance to fight for their freedom. They were stuck. Then God sent Moses. After many miracles and plagues sent by God, Pharaoh finally agreed to let Moses and the children of Israel leave Egypt forever. As they traveled, they came to the edge of the Red Sea. Just as they were wondering what to do next, the army of Pharaoh came over the horizon to kill them. There was sand to their right, sand to their left, an angry army behind them, and a giant sea in front of them. They were stuck. Then Moses spoke for God.

"Fear ye not, stand still, and see the salvation of the Lord . . . the Lord shall fight for you." (Exodus 14:13–14)

Immediately, an angel of God created a protective barrier of clouds between the Israelites and the Egyptian army. Under God's direction, Moses stretched his hand over the waters and a powerful wind came and blew all through the night. The sea opened to the left and to the right, and the children of Israel walked through the passageway on dry ground. God had delivered them.

There will be times in your life when you will have problems to your left, to your right, behind you, and in front of you. You will wonder what to do. Don't fear. Stand still and watch. If you are faithful, God will deliver you as He did the people of Moses.

? Will you look to God in times of trouble? Will you listen for His reassurance and His direction when you need to be rescued?

Activity

Review the whole story of Moses's life (by reading it or watching a movie depiction) and look for times when the Lord delivered Moses or the children of Israel. List how many different ways God delivered His people. Talk about how He can deliver people today.

Book of Exodus
Pharaoh

The family of Jacob (Israel) moved to Egypt when Joseph was a ruler over the nation and worked for a trusting pharaoh. After hundreds of years and many other pharaohs, a new king of Egypt, or pharaoh, started to reign. He was afraid of how many Israelites there were, fearing they would overtake his rule. He made them slaves and gave them difficult work to try to control them. When their numbers still continued to increase, he ordered the midwives to kill all Israelite baby boys when they were born. When they secretly refused, he ordered all of his people to throw any Israelite baby boys into the river. Moses escaped this fate and was miraculously raised by Pharaoh's daughter. When Moses killed an Egyptian taskmaster in defense of a slave, Pharaoh sentenced Moses to death. Moses ran away, but he returned forty years later with a message from God: let the Israelites go free. Pharaoh refused. Even after nine plagues sent by God, Pharaoh refused. The tenth plague killed every firstborn son in Egypt, including Pharaoh's son. He finally let the people go, but he changed his mind soon after they left. Pharaoh and his armies were drowned in the Red Sea when they tried to kill the Israelites.

 Many Bible scholars believe the pharaoh in this story was Ramses II, but no one is completely sure.

 The pharaohs in Egypt considered themselves representatives of the Egyptian gods they believed in.

 The magicians and wise men of Pharaoh were able to imitate some of the miracles Moses performed, which made Pharaoh not want to let the Israelites go.

 The events surrounding the final plague that convinced Pharaoh to let the Israelites go are often referred to as the Passover.

 "And Pharaoh said, Who is the Lord, that I should obey his voice to let Israel go? I know not the Lord, neither will I let Israel go" (Exodus 5:2).

A Heart of Stone (Exodus 7–14)

When Moses first came to Pharaoh to deliver the message from God to let His people go free, Pharaoh was very angry. Time after time, Moses came to Pharaoh with the same message from the Lord: let His people go. Each time he asked, Pharaoh refused. The Lord began to send many plagues upon Pharaoh and Egypt to convince the king that Moses's message truly was from God.

"And the heart of Pharaoh was hardened, and he did not let the people go." (Exodus 9:7)

The waters turned to blood; hundreds of frogs, lice, locusts, and flies infested people's houses, cupboards, and clothes; the cattle died; people got open sores all over their skin; the heavens rained down huge hailstones and fire; and the whole land was covered in darkness for three days. Pharaoh still refused! Every time a plague came to Egypt, Pharaoh would promise to let the people go if the plague went away. Once it went away, he changed his mind again and refused to release the people. The solution to the problem was simple, but Pharaoh kept hardening his heart and brought heartache, pain, and sadness to himself and everyone in his kingdom.

Sometimes we know what is right, but we are too stubborn to admit it or to change. Our stubbornness makes things bad or worse for us, and it drags other people down with us.

? Will you be humble when you realize you are wrong and make the decision to change? Will you notice the effects of your decisions on the people around you?

Activity

Prepare a delicious drink and pour everyone a glass. Then put a drop or two of vinegar or vegetable oil in it. Have them taste it, and explain how one person's decisions can ruin things for everyone else. Talk about how this lesson applies to families, friends, classes, and communities.

Book of Numbers

Joshua & Caleb

 After the children of Israel left Egypt, they wandered in the Sinai wilderness for forty years. During the Israelites' wanderings, the Lord commanded Moses to send twelve spies into the promised land of Canaan and bring back a report to the rest of the people. Moses selected one person from each tribe, including Joshua from the tribe of Ephraim and Caleb from the tribe of Judah. The group of spies spent forty days scouting things out in the land of Canaan. They all returned with negative reports except for Joshua and Caleb. At the end of the forty years in the wilderness, Joshua was called to be the new prophet and leader of the Israelites after Moses died. Caleb continued to stand by and support him. Joshua led the children of Israel through the Jordan River, which opened like the Red Sea, and led them to conquer the land that God had promised to them. Both Joshua and Caleb were dedicated to the Lord and always looked to Him for answers to the challenges they faced.

 Moses changed Joshua's name from Oshea to Joshua. Joshua means "God is help" or "God is salvation." The name Joshua is also the Hebrew translation of the name Jesus.

 Caleb and Joshua both lived in Egypt as slaves before following Moses into the wilderness. They were the only two adults who came out of Egypt, passed through the Red Sea, and also entered the promised land of Canaan.

 Joshua and Caleb were both brilliant military leaders. Joshua led the children of Israel in a famous battle against the city of Jericho.

 Caleb inherited the land of Hebron in the promised land, and his family lived there through the time of King David. Hebron is believed by many to be the burial place of Abraham, Isaac, and Jacob.

 "[Joshua and Caleb] spake unto all . . . If the Lord delight in us, then he will bring us into this land, and give it us . . . rebel not ye against the Lord, neither fear ye" (Numbers 14:7–9).

Wholly Devoted (Numbers 13–14)

The children of Israel escaped Egypt and knew that God was leading them to a promised land. When Moses's spies returned, they came back with bunches of grapes and stories of beautiful places. They also came back with doubt. Ten of the spies convinced the rest of the group that they could never go into that land. They said it was filled with giants and danger and that going there would lead to their death. The children of Israel began to rise up in hysterical rebellion against Moses and the Lord. Caleb and Joshua stood up in Moses's defense. Their stories and reports were about hope, opportunities, and God's blessings. The people picked up rocks to throw at Caleb and Joshua, but they stood by their report and the Lord. The Lord said:

"But my servant Caleb, because he had another spirit with him, and hath followed me fully, him will I bring into the land." (Numbers 14:24)

Caleb and Joshua were the only adults who left Egypt that were allowed to enter the promised land. They experienced the same hardships and fears as the rest of the Israelites in the wilderness, but they chose to give their whole hearts over to God. Everything they did was with a heart that was wholly devoted. Their belief and complete devotion to God brought them great blessings, allowed them to see hope and possibilities when others saw doubt, and inspired the next generation.

We can choose whether to approach our journey in life like the ten spies—doubtful, partial, and rebellious—or like Joshua and Caleb—wholly devoted.

? Are you wholly devoted to God? Have you decided to "follow Him fully"?

Activity

Draw a line on the sidewalk or in the dirt or sand. Have everyone stand on one side and then ask anyone who is committed to being wholly devoted to God step across. As people step across, ask each person to say at least one thing he or she will do, say, or believe to show commitment to following Him fully.

Book of Numbers
Balaam & the Donkey

 Balaam was a man who lived near the land of Canaan. Many people believed he had the power to bless and curse people. As the children of Israel journeyed through the wilderness for forty years, they interacted and battled with many other civilizations they passed by. The Lord strengthened the children of Israel, and they quickly gained a reputation for being a mighty people. A man named Balak, the king of the Moabites, was afraid of the Israelites and wanted someone to curse them so they would be weak. He knew of Balaam and tried to hire him to curse Israel so that Balak's armies could defeat them. Balaam turned down the money at first, but eventually he agreed to go and curse Israel. The Lord was angry with Balaam and spoke through a donkey to convince him not to follow through with his plan. Balaam pronounced a blessing on Israel instead of a curse.

 Balak felt threatened by the Israelites when they were camped on the border of Canaan at the Jordan River. It was near the end of their forty years of wandering.

 Balaam traveled hundreds of miles to meet Balak and to curse Israel.

 The Bible calls Balaam a prophet, but it is not the same as prophets of the Lord. He did not lead people to believe in Jesus Christ. Another word for a prophet like Balaam is a soothsayer.

 Balaam was killed in a battle between the Midianites and the Israelites only a short time after these events.

 "Which have forsaken the right way, and are gone astray, following the way of Balaam, the son of Bosor, who loved the wages of unrighteousness" (2 Peter 2:15–16).

Out of the Mouth of Donkeys (Numbers 22)

It must have been difficult to turn down Balak's treasure. When Balaam finally gave in to Balak's requests, the Lord wanted to stop him from doing something he would regret, so He sent an angel with a sword to block Balaam's way. Balaam could not see the angel, but his donkey could. Realizing the danger ahead, the donkey tried three times to stop Balaam from going forward. She walked off into a field, smashed his foot against a wall, and eventually just lay down on the road and didn't budge. Each time, Balaam got angry and hit his donkey to get her to move. The Lord opened the mouth of the donkey and she talked to Balaam, asking him why he was hitting her. "Have I not been a good donkey for many years?" she asked. She was only trying to help!

"Then the Lord opened the eyes of Balaam, and he saw the angel of the Lord standing in the way, and his sword drawn in his hand: and he bowed down his head." (Numbers 22:31)

Balaam finally realized he was doing something wrong and followed what the Lord wanted Him to do.

Sometimes we are like Balaam, and other times we are like the donkey. Often, like Balaam, we cannot see when we are heading in the wrong direction or down a path of spiritual danger. When family and friends try to warn us, we get angry until we eventually understand they are trying to help. When we are like the donkey and see the spiritual danger ahead, it can be hard to try to help people when they react with anger or hurtful words.

? Will you listen to and trust your family, leaders, and friends when they speak up to try to help? Will you speak up when you need to, even if there is a risk of an angry reaction?

Activity

Discuss a few scenarios in which we should speak up to prevent someone else from doing something he or she would regret. For example, what would you say if you found out your friend stole something from a store? Take turns role-playing and practicing ways to speak up.

Book of Joshua
Rahab

 One of the most famous battles of the Old Testament is the battle of Jericho, when the walls came tumbling down. Rahab lived in a house right on the edge of one of the walls of the city. She was known in the city as an unrighteous woman with a bad reputation. The Lord commanded Joshua to conquer and destroy the city of Jericho, but before the battle, Joshua sent two spies into Jericho to develop a plan. Rahab hid the spies in her home and helped them escape when they were discovered by the king. She saved their lives. As a trade, the spies promised to save anyone who was in her home on the day they destroyed the city. She was instructed to hang a red cord from her window as a signal of which house was hers. She brought her father, mother, and her extended family into the house. The only survivors from the battle of Jericho were Rahab and her family. She joined with the children of Israel and lived among them the rest of her life.

 The battle of Jericho was won after the soldiers and priests of Joshua walked around the city for seven days. On the seventh day, they blew their trumpets and the walls of the city miraculously came down.

 Rahab married an Israelite man named Salmon. Many scholars believe he was one of the spies sent to scout out the city.

 King David is the great-great-grandson of Rahab. Ruth was her daughter-in-law.

 Only four women are mentioned in the genealogy of Christ in the New Testament. Rahab is one of them.

 "And Joshua saved Rahab . . . and her father's household, and all that she had; and she dwelleth in Israel even unto this day; because she hid the messengers, which Joshua sent to spy out Jericho" (Joshua 6:25).

A Red Thread (Joshua 2)

The two Israelite spies were hiding in the roof of Rahab's house when the soldiers came looking for them. Rahab had just met the spies, but surprisingly she decided to lie to the soldiers of her own king to save the lives of strangers. When the soldiers left, Rahab shared her reasons with the spies. She had heard stories of these men before they came, and she believed the Lord was on their side.

"And as soon as we had heard these things, our hearts did melt . . . for the Lord your God, he is God in heaven above, and in earth beneath." (Joshua 2:11)

Rahab had not been a righteous woman before, but once she had a chance to meet and learn from the spies, she accepted the truth, changed her life completely, and never went back to her old ways. The night of the battle of Jericho, Rahab hung a red thread in her window as a signal to Joshua's army that she had saved the spies. The house with the red thread was passed over, and the people in it were saved from death.

Sometimes we do things that are not right in God's eyes and we live with sin. Like Rahab, though, we can change. When we truly change, or repent, forgiveness comes and the eternal consequences pass over us. The Savior's blood, as red as Rahab's thread, can cleanse us and save us. He is the one who brings the change.

? When you make mistakes, will you look to the Savior for help to change? Will you recognize your wrongs and make the change as quickly as Rahab?

Activity

Learn about the Savior's forgiveness by reading Isaiah 1:18–19 together. Have everyone cut a red thread or yarn to hang somewhere in their room as a reminder of His mercy and our ability to change quickly.

Book of Judges
Deborah

 During the time between the children of Israel entering the promised land and the reign of their first king, Saul, the leaders of the people were called judges. During this time, there were twelve main judges of Israel. Deborah, the prophetess, was the fourth judge and the only female judge that is mentioned in the Bible. During her time as a judge, the children of Israel lived wickedly and were conquered by a neighboring people called the Canaanites. The Canaanite military leader, Sisera, had a very large army. Deborah called upon a man named Barak to lead the armies of Israel in a battle against Sisera. Deborah testified to him that the Lord would fight for them. The Lord strengthened their army, and they won! The Israelites were rescued from the Canaanites and then began to follow God again.

 Deborah is called "the wife of Lapidoth" in the Bible. This phrase has also been translated from Hebrew by some scholars as "a woman with a torch-like spirit."

 Sisera had 900 chariots in his army in the battle against Barak and Deborah. The miraculous flooding of a nearby river helped the Israelites win the battle.

 Deborah would often wait under a palm tree for the people in Israel to come to her to ask for help with their struggles.

 Miriam, the sister of Moses, was also referred to as a prophetess. A prophetess is a female who has the spirit of prophecy. The book of Revelation describes the spirit of prophecy as the testimony of Jesus (see Revelation 19:10).

 "And Deborah said unto Barak, Up; for this is the day in which the Lord hath delivered Sisera into thine hand: is not the Lord gone out before thee?" (Judges 4:14).

With a Torch-like Spirit (Judges 4–5)

The Canaanite leader Sisera was a mighty military man with a very large army. Even though the Lord commanded the children of Israel to fight for their freedom, their leader Barak and others were frightened and did not think they could win. Deborah trusted God. Her confidence in the Lord gave Barak and the army of Israel great courage and strength. When she instructed him to go up to battle, Barak pled with her to come with him.

"If thou wilt go with me, then I will go: but if thou wilt not go with me, then I will not go." (Judges 4:8)

There was something about Deborah that gave Barak the confidence to do something hard. He knew that if she was there, he would not fail. Deborah, the woman with the torch-like spirit, fanned the flames of his faith. The battle was a success, and the Lord delivered the children of Israel once again, this time through the hands of a woman.

There are many people who know what the Lord wants them to do but hesitate because of fear. They forget about His promises or do not have a firm enough trust in Him. Your faith and trust in God can inspire others to do what they are nervous or afraid to do. Your torch-like spirit can light the faith of others.

? Will you stand by others when their faith seems weak? Will you encourage and remind people about the power of God and His presence in their lives?

Activity

Give everyone a candle and have them stand near one another. Light one candle. Ask the person holding that candle to say something encouraging to someone else and then to light that person's candle with his or her own. Keep doing this until everyone's candle is lit. Discuss how we can give each other strength.

Gideon

Book of Judges

Gideon became one of the ruling judges of Israel. An enemy nation, the Midianites, had conquered Israel and controlled them for seven years. The Israelites were very poor and prayed to the Lord for a deliverer. The Lord heard their prayer and called Gideon, then a simple farmer. An angel came to call Gideon to lead an army that would deliver Israel from the Midianites. Gideon did not think he was the right person for the job. He considered himself too weak and unimportant for the job. The Lord performed miracles for Gideon to convince him that he was the right one. Gideon's most famous feat is when he led an army of only 300 men against a great and large army of Midianites and defeated them, driving them out of their land. The children of Israel started worshipping the Lord again after the battle, but unfortunately, after Gideon died they returned to their wicked ways.

 After Gideon defeated the Midianites the children of Israel tried to make him king, but he refused.

 Gideon was from the tribe of Manasseh. He thought it was one of the weakest of all the tribes.

 Not a single member of Gideon's army of 300 died in the battle against the Midianites. In fact, none of them even lifted a sword.

 "And the angel of the Lord appeared unto him, and said unto him, The Lord is with thee, thou mighty man of valour" (Judges 6:12).

Trumpets, Pitchers, and Torches (Judges 6–8)

When the Lord called Gideon to lead an army against the Midianites, Gideon gathered a group of 32,000 men to fight. The Lord then told him to send home anyone who was afraid. Only 10,000 men remained. The Lord then told him the army was still too big. Gideon led the army to a river for a drink. Anyone who drank the water like a dog would go home, and anyone who cupped the water to his mouth would stay. After the drink, only 300 men remained. When Gideon saw the small size of his army, he looked again to the Lord for help. Following the Lord's instructions, each man was given a trumpet, an empty pitcher, and a lamp. They surrounded the Midianites at night and on command each man blew his trumpet, smashed his pitcher, held up his lamp, and yelled,

"The sword of the Lord, and of Gideon." (Judges 7:20)

The Midianites were confused, thought they were outnumbered, and scrambled and ran out of the lands of Israel. The battle was a victory! Gideon had thought he was too weak of a leader and that his army was too small, but the Lord led him and gave him the right tools to win the fight.

Sometimes we will feel too small for something we are asked to do—even things that the Lord asks us to do. You might have a person to help or a mission to complete that you don't feel you can accomplish. On those occasions, the Lord will give you what you need and teach you what to do to lead you to victory.

? Will you look to the Lord for guidance when you have a difficult task in front of you? Will you trust His guidance when it comes and do things His way?

Activity

Gather a trumpet, an empty pitcher, and a lamp. Discuss what each of the three items could represent as tools the Lord has given us in our day to fight our battles. (Example: Could the lamp be faith?)

Samson

Book of Judges

Samson lived during the time of the judges and led the people for twenty years as one of the twelve judges. Samson's mother could not have any children for a long time, but God promised her she would have a miracle son. An angel came and commanded her to raise her son as a Nazarite. Nazarites were people who made certain promises and lived in a certain way to show their devotion to the Lord. This included not eating grapes and never cutting their hair. Samson was given mighty strength as long as he never broke his vows. Samson did many foolish things during his life because of his strength, but despite his weaknesses, God still used him to begin to save the children of Israel from an enemy nation, the Philistines. At the end of his life, Samson broke his vows, lost his strength, and the Philistines captured him and made him blind. God gave him strength one last time to show the Philistines who the true God was. Samson knocked down their temple to the false god Dagon, but he also died in the collapse. The Philistines continued to be a great problem for the Israelites.

 At one time, Samson faced an army of 1,000 Philistines and won. His only weapon was the jawbone of a donkey.

 Samson was from the tribe of Dan.

 When Samson was on his way to his wedding, he saved his family from a lion that attacked them on the road. He tore it in half!

 The Israelites had been in bondage to the Philistines for forty years when Samson was born.

 "For lo, thou shalt . . . bear a son; and no razor shall come on his head: for the child shall be a Nazarite unto God from the womb: and he shall begin to deliver Israel out of the hand of the Philistines" (Judges 13:5).

Keep Your Guard Up (Judges 13–16)

Despite Samson's weaknesses, God blessed him with amazing gifts and used him as an instrument in His hands to do His work. Samson's enemies knew how powerful and strong he was and wanted to do everything they could to stop him. The Philistines tried many different ways to capture and defeat Samson, but as long as he kept his vows, the Lord gave him strength to escape. Then he met Delilah. Delilah was a beautiful Philistine woman who tricked Samson into thinking she was his friend. Delilah would beg Samson to tell her the secret of his strength. Samson lied to her and told her different ways he would lose his strength. Delilah would try them, but Samson would defeat the armies when they came. This happened three different times.

"And it came to pass, when she pressed him daily with her words, and urged him, so that his soul was vexed unto death; that he told her." (Judges 16:16–17)

Samson gave in after continual and constant pressing and told Delilah his secret when she promised again she would not tell anyone. That night, Delilah cut Samson's hair, which broke his vow. Sadly, he lost his strength and was captured and died in Philistine chains.

Samson is not very different from us. God has given us mighty gifts to do his work. Enemies to righteousness and goodness know about our strengths. They will try persistently and continually to stop us. They will try to get us to break our vows with God to leave us weak.

? Will you keep your guard up every day, keep your promises, and be diligent in the work that God has for you to do?

Activity

Play Kick the Can (look up the instructions online if you need to). Talk about how the person who is "it" has to be diligent and watchful to win the game. Explain how we need the same amount of diligence as we fight to keep our vows against those who want us to break them.

Book of Ruth

Ruth

 The story of Ruth is sandwiched between the stories of deliverance in the book of Judges and the calling of Samuel the prophet. The book of Ruth departs from the storyline of the children of Israel and focuses on one particular important family. Ruth was a woman from Moab who married a man named Mahlon from the city of Bethlehem. Mahlon; his brother, Chilion; their mother, Naomi; and their father, Elimelech; had moved to Moab when there was a great famine in their homeland. Naomi's two sons cared for their mother after their father died. The two sons married Moabite women, Ruth and Orpah. After several years, the two brothers died and left Naomi, Ruth, and Orpah all alone. Naomi went to live in Bethlehem, and Ruth decided to go with her to care for her. In Bethlehem, Ruth met a man named Boaz, who was very kind and allowed her to pick food from his fields. He even encouraged his servants to drop some food on purpose for her to gather. With the encouragement of Naomi, Ruth married Boaz, and he cared for Ruth and Naomi the rest of their lives.

 Ruth's first husband, Mahlon, and her second husband, Boaz, were both from the tribe of Judah.

 Ruth and Boaz are the great-grandparents of David, the future king of Israel.

 Moab was a country neighboring Israel. At times the Moabites were enemies to the Israelites. Many of the Moabites were descendants of Lot.

 Both King David and Jesus Christ were born in Bethlehem. Ruth is one of the four women who is mentioned in the genealogy of Jesus.

 "It hath fully been shewed me, all that thou hast done unto thy mother in law . . . the Lord recompense thy work, and a full reward be given thee of the Lord God of Israel, under whose wings thou art come to trust" (Ruth 2:11–12).

My People (Ruth 1–4)

For ten years Ruth was married and lived a happy life with her husband, mother-in-law, and other family members. She lived near extended family in a place that was very familiar and comfortable. Then all of that changed. When her husband and her brother-in-law died, Ruth, Orpah, and Naomi were left alone to find a way to survive. Naomi, Ruth's mother-in-law, decided it was best to move back to Bethlehem. She insisted that Orpah and Ruth stay in Moab to try to find new husbands and start a new life. Ruth would not think of it.

"Entreat me not to leave thee, or to return from following after thee: for whither thou goest, I will go; and where thou lodgest, I will lodge: thy people shall be my people, and thy God my God." (Ruth 1:16)

Ruth decided to stick with her family. This meant that she would leave the place she knew and the people and culture she loved. This also meant that she would need to work hard to take care of her mother-in-law. Her kindness was noticed by Boaz. He was amazed that she would be so loyal and gentle and good to her mother-in-law. Ruth's kindness and loyalty to her family led to great blessings for all of them through the rest of their lives.

God has placed us all in families. During life, hard times will come to members of our families. We can be like Ruth and stand by them with loyalty and kindness for our whole lives. The way we treat and care for our families will determine the happiness and blessings we enjoy in our homes and throughout our lives.

? Will you practice fierce loyalty to your family? Will you show them love and kindness through your thoughts, words, and actions?

Activity

Each night of the week, pray for the members of your family by name. Thank God for their gifts and the blessings they bring into your life. Pray for ways to show loyalty to them. Watch what this simple act does to the feeling in your home.

Book of 1 Samuel
Samuel

 Samuel was a marvelous leader and a courageous prophet. He is considered the last of all of the judges. Hannah, his mother, prayed for God to send her a child and made a promise that she would dedicate the child's life to the Lord. God sent her Samuel. When he was old enough, Samuel went to live and serve in the sanctuary with Eli, the high priest. From a very young age, Samuel showed patience, devotion, and love for the Lord and the people. God called Samuel as His spokesman when he was quite young. Samuel served as a judge and spiritual leader of Israel for many decades. When he was older, the people did not want to have him as their leader anymore and demanded a king. Even though the Lord counseled against it, the people insisted, and the Lord directed Samuel to choose King Saul. Samuel also anointed David as the future king while Saul was still reigning. When Samuel died, the people mourned greatly. He was courageous in battle, stood up for God and truth at every opportunity, and loved the people enough to lead them to righteousness.

 Samuel went to serve with Eli in the sanctuary once he was old enough to leave his mother. Every year she visited him and brought him a new coat.

 The sanctuary where Samuel served as a boy housed the ark of the covenant. It was considered the throne seat of the Lord. It held the tablets from Sinai inside and was very special and sacred.

 Samuel also led the people of Israel in war. In one battle, the Philistines attacked, and the Lord sent a mighty thunderstorm to assist the Israelites in winning the war at a place called Ebenezer.

 "And Samuel grew, and the Lord was with him, and did let none of his words fall to the ground. And all Israel from Dan even to Beer-sheba knew that Samuel was established to be a prophet of the Lord" (1 Samuel 3:19–20).

Listen (1 Samuel 3)

When Samuel began his service in the sanctuary, things had not been going the way the Lord wanted them to. Eli, the high priest, had two sons who were very wicked and treated the sacred places of the temple very poorly. Their father knew of these things and told his sons to stop, but he did not follow through and ultimately allowed them to continue. Samuel served faithfully and righteously and did not follow the example of the older boys. One night, Samuel was sleeping and the Lord called his name. Samuel thought it was Eli, so he got out of bed and went to see what he needed. Eli told Samuel that he had been asleep and hadn't called Samuel, so Samuel went back to bed. The Lord called Samuel's name again, and once more Samuel went to Eli's room to see what he needed. Eli sent him back to bed a second time. Once again the Lord called Samuel's name, and he went to the bedside of Eli for the third time. This time, Eli realized it was the Lord calling Samuel.

"Go, lie down: and it shall be, if he call thee, that thou shalt say, Speak Lord; for thy servant heareth." (1 Samuel 3:9)

Samuel did just what Eli said to do, and the Lord spoke with Samuel and delivered to him the first of many messages in his life. He learned to hear the voice of the Lord and obey.

The Lord wants to speak to us and direct us as well. Sometimes we hear His words with our ears, and sometimes we hear them with our heart. Just like Samuel, we might not recognize the Lord speaking to us if we are not listening for Him. Sometimes we need others to teach us how to hear His voice.

? Will you listen for the words and the directions of the Lord in your life? What message does He have for you today?

Activity

Have everyone close their eyes. While their eyes are closed, play a song. At some point during the song, ring a quiet bell. At the end of the song ask everyone if they heard the bell. Then have them close their eyes and listen a second time, but this time tell them to listen for the bell. Discuss how we can listen for the Lord's voice.

Book of 1 Samuel
King Saul

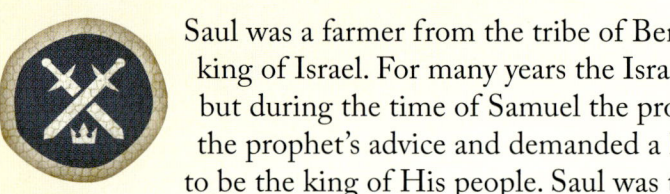 Saul was a farmer from the tribe of Benjamin who became the first king of Israel. For many years the Israelites did not have a king, but during the time of Samuel the prophet, they went against the prophet's advice and demanded a king. The Lord chose Saul to be the king of His people. Saul was tall and handsome and an amazing soldier. The new kingdom of Israel was in terrible trouble when Saul became the king. Israel's enemies, particularly the Philistines, were close to completely destroying the entire nation. Saul fought valiantly his whole time as king to protect and establish the kingdom. At the beginning of his reign, he followed the Lord and His commands. By the end, Saul was disobedient and fell out of favor with God. King Saul died in a battle against the Philistines that he should not have entered. Even though Saul brought great strength to Israel during his reign, the final battle of Saul's life left Israel in worse condition than when Saul had first become king.

 King Saul was married and had five children—three sons and two daughters.

 Jonathan, Saul's oldest son, was a valiant warrior and dear friend of future King David.

 Michal, Saul's youngest daughter, married the future King David. David became Saul's son-in-law.

 Most Bible scholars think Saul ruled as king around 1020 to 1010 BC.

 "And he had a son, whose name was Saul, a choice young man, and a goodly: and there was not among the children of Israel a goodlier person than he: from his shoulders and upward he was higher than any of the people" (1 Samuel 8:2).

Green with the Envy Blues (1 Samuel 18–26)

Saul was a mighty warrior and a courageous king of Israel. The more he defeated the Philistines in battle, the more the people loved and admired him. One day, Saul chose a young man named David to be his armor bearer. David became a strong soldier and did remarkable things in battles—including killing a Philistine giant named Goliath. Saul was impressed and made David the leader of his armies. The people started to praise David and love him for all of the great things he did. They sang songs about Saul, but they sang even more praising ones about David.

"And Saul was very wroth, and the saying displeased him; and he said, they have ascribed unto David ten thousands, and to me they have ascribed but thousands." (1 Samuel 18:8)

From that time on, Saul started to hate David. He sent David into battles he thought he would lose, but David always came out a hero—bigger and better each time. Even though this was good for Saul's kingdom, it made Saul's anger and jealousy grow each time. Saul spent many of his years as king trying to hunt down David and kill him. He even killed people that tried to help David escape. Even though David was his son's best friend and his son-in-law, Saul's once-good heart became filled with jealousy and caused him to make terrible mistakes and eventually die a sad and lonely man.

Jealousy is an easy "disease" to catch. It causes us to forget the great things God has done for us and turns us against people who love us and are our friends. It can cause people to do terrible things. Unlike Saul, we can protect our hearts against being jealous about the good things in other people's lives.

? Will you look for the good in other people and strive to be happy for the good things that they accomplish? Will you avoid comparing yourself to other people?

Activity

Make a list of five people you know and admire. Choose one (or more) to write a letter to, and tell the person what you love and admire about him or her.

Book of 1 Samuel

King David

King David is considered the greatest king of Israel and was the king during the golden era of the nation. Under his reign, Israel's greatest enemies, the Philistines, were finally defeated. Israel became a united and powerful kingdom, and their land expanded farther than it had before. David was the eighth and youngest son of Jesse, a sheepherder from Bethlehem. Samuel the prophet chose and anointed David as the new king in a secret ceremony while King Saul was still the acting king. David became famous in Israel when he killed Goliath, a giant Philistine warrior, in a miraculous battle with a stone and a sling. He became close friends with Prince Jonathan, the son of King Saul, and he married Michal, the princess. Even though they were family, Saul became jealous of David, so David spent many years hiding from the king. When Saul died, David became the recognized king of Israel and began to defeat their enemies and expand the land. David moved the capital city to Jerusalem during his reign. David is considered by many to be one of the most important people in Israel's history.

 David was from the tribe of Judah and was the descendant of Ruth and Boaz. He is an ancestor of Jesus Christ, who was also born in Bethlehem about 1000 years later.

 Goliath, the Philistine giant that David defeated, was over nine feet tall and wore armor weighing over 125 pounds.

 About half of the psalms in the Old Testament are believed to be written by King David. He was a gifted harpist and musician.

 David bought the land and organized the plans for the building of the temple in Jerusalem. His son Solomon actually built the temple. It was built at the same place that Abraham took Isaac to be sacrificed.

 "Then said David to the Philistine, Thou comest to me with a sword, and with a spear, and with a shield: but I come to thee in the name of the Lord of hosts, the God of the armies of Israel" (1 Samuel 17:45).

On the Inside (1 Samuel 16)

Once King Saul began to make unrighteous choices as the leader of Israel, the Lord commanded Samuel the prophet to go choose another king for His people. One morning, the Lord sent Samuel to the house of Jesse from Bethlehem to find the future king among his sons. Jesse brought out his seven oldest sons to meet Samuel. As each boy passed, Samuel was more and more certain that each son was the one God would choose. They were tall and strong and handsome and had the look of a king. But one by one, God whispered in Samuel's ear that the future king was not one of those impressive boys. Surprised, Samuel asked if there were any others. There was another. David, the youngest son, had been left out tending the sheep. No one imagined he would be the future king.

"But the Lord said unto Samuel, Look not on his countenance, or on the height of his stature . . . for the Lord seeth not as man seeth; for man looketh on the outward appearance, but the Lord looketh on the heart." (1 Samuel 16:7)

No one imagined that boy would slay a giant and save all of Israel. No one imagined he would unite the tribes and become the nation's greatest leader. No one imagined the young shepherd and obscure Bethlehemite boy would be the ancestor of the King of kings.

Man still looks on the outside and God still looks on the heart. We never know when we look at someone what God sees on the inside. Others don't know what God sees in you.

? Will you leave final judgments to God? Will you try to see and treat people the way that He does?

Activity

Wrap up several gifts—some nice ones and some gag gifts. Put the best and nicest presents in the ugliest wrapping. Wrap up the gag gifts beautifully. Have everyone choose a gift and open it. Review the lesson from the life of David—the humble farmer boy who became Israel's golden king.

King Solomon

Book of 1 Kings

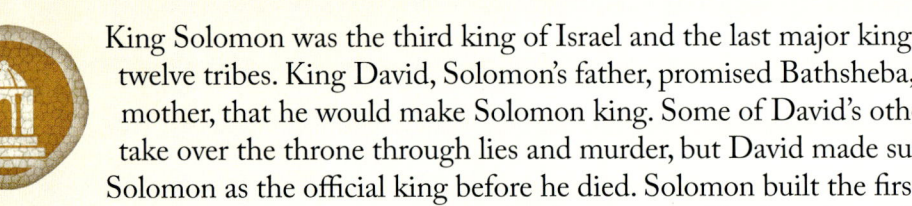 King Solomon was the third king of Israel and the last major king of the united twelve tribes. King David, Solomon's father, promised Bathsheba, Solomon's mother, that he would make Solomon king. Some of David's other sons tried to take over the throne through lies and murder, but David made sure to announce Solomon as the official king before he died. Solomon built the first permanent temple in Jerusalem on the land his father had bought for that purpose. The kingdom of Israel was very rich and powerful during the days of King Solomon. He organized the kingdom into twelve districts and collected heavy taxes from the people to fund all of his buildings and projects. Solomon traded with many neighboring nations, and his reputation of wealth and wisdom started to spread through the ancient world. His building projects grew out of control, and many of the people did not like him because of the heavy taxes he required from them. His son, Rehoboam, demanded even more taxes than his father when he became king. This led to the splitting of the kingdom. Solomon started out as a righteous king, but unfortunately due to his pride he started to live wickedly at the end of his life.

 King Solomon ruled as king of Israel for forty years from about 970 to 930 BC.

 The temple of Solomon took seven years to build. It was built from the finest materials Solomon could obtain, including the gold that covered the walls. Over 150,000 workers built the temple.

 Solomon was known as the wisest man who ever lived. Most of the proverbs in the Old Testament are attributed to him.

 Solomon built many other expensive buildings in Jerusalem, including his own home, which took thirteen years to build.

 "Among many nations was there no king like him, who was beloved of his God, and God made him king over all Israel: nevertheless even him did outlandish women cause to sin" (Nehemiah 13:26).

The Greatest Gifts (1 Kings 3)

King Solomon was only twenty years old when he became king, which even he considered to be quite young. His father had been a mighty and powerful king, and Solomon was intimidated to be the next king in line. He turned to the Lord in great humility for help. He tried to live as close to the Lord's commandments as he could. One night, an angel appeared to Solomon in a dream to deliver a message from God. The angel told Solomon that whatever he wanted, God would give him. Without hesitation, Solomon answered.

"Give therefore thy servant an understanding heart to judge thy people, that I may discern between good and bad." (1 Kings 3:9)

The Lord was pleased with Solomon and gave him what his heart wanted—the understanding between good and bad. He also blessed Solomon with more riches and honors than any other king. Many people came to Solomon to get advice for their problems. Perhaps the most famous example is when he determined which of two fighting women was the real mother of a baby (see 1 Kings 3: 16–27). All of Israel knew how wise Solomon was. Solomon avoided a lot of trouble and became a great blessing in many people's lives because of his understanding heart.

God is very concerned about the desires of our hearts. He is the giver of all gifts. One of the greatest gifts we can ask for is the gift of an understanding heart—to know the difference between good and bad. This is a gift and blessing we could all use in our lives.

? Will you seek and pray for an understanding heart? Will you look to God for help in determining the difference between good and bad?

Activity

Find a genie's lamp (or a picture of one). Pass it around and have everyone say three wishes they would wish for. Talk about what those wishes could do for their life. Then discuss what good could come if they wished for an understanding heart.

Book of 1 Kings

King Jehoshaphat

After the reign of King Solomon, the kingdom of Israel divided into two separate kingdoms—one of them named Israel (with ten tribes) and the other named Judah (with two tribes—Judah and Benjamin). Jehoshaphat was the fourth king of Judah, the southern kingdom. He and his father before him were righteous kings. He was king of Judah while King Ahab was king of Israel, the northern kingdom. Jehoshaphat continued an effort to help people return to religious practice and belief in God that his father started at the end of his life. He sent prophets and men of God among the people to teach them about God's laws. He broke down false temples and other buildings built for wicked purposes. He appointed priests and family heads in all of the cities to help people remember the Lord and to help them solve their problems peacefully. He established strong military posts to defend his kingdom and formed a peaceful alliance with the northern kingdom of Israel. He looked to God to help him as king, and even his enemies admired him. His own people brought him tributes throughout his life which made him very rich. When he died, he was buried in Jerusalem in great honor.

 Jehoshaphat died when he was about sixty years old.

 He reigned as king of Judah for about 25 years, around 872 to 848 BC.

 Jehoshaphat is an ancestor of Joseph, the husband of Mary and earthly father of Jesus Christ.

 The writers of the Chronicles in the Old Testament praised Jehoshaphat as a righteous and powerful king of Judah and placed him in a position of honor with King Hezekiah and King Josiah.

 "And the Lord was with Jehoshaphat, because he walked in the first ways of his father David. . . . Therefore the Lord stablished the kingdom in his hand; and all Judah brought to Jehoshaphat presents; and he had riches and honour in abundance. And his heart was lifted up in the ways of the Lord" (2 Chronicles 17:3, 5–6).

What Shall We Do? (1 Kings 22)

Jehoshaphat's father, King Asa of Judah, did not get along with the northern kingdom of Israel. When Jehoshaphat became king, he decided to mend the broken relationship and become allies with his neighboring kingdom. King Ahab of Israel had been fighting against Syria for three years. He sent a letter to Jehoshaphat and asked him for help in the battle. As a sign of friendship, Jehoshaphat agreed and gathered his armies. As they got ready for the battle, King Ahab gathered 400 of his counselors and wise men and asked them for advice in the fight. He asked them to prophesy about the outcome of the war. They all promised success. When they were finished, Jehoshaphat stood to speak.

"And Jehoshaphat said, Is there not here a prophet of the Lord besides, that we may inquire of him?" (1 Kings 22:7)

Jehoshaphat wanted to know what the Lord would say through His holy prophets. Ahab told his new ally about a prophet named Micaiah, whom he didn't like very much. Micaiah always seemed to tell Ahab what he didn't want to hear. Jehoshaphat insisted that a servant invite the prophet of God to their camp before they went into battle. Micaiah came and prophesied the will of the Lord to the kings. As Ahab had feared, Micaiah told them that they would win the war, but that if Ahab fought, he would die in the fight. Ahab ignored the advice, and the two kings went into battle with great assurance. Sure enough, it came to pass just as the Lord had prophesied through Micaiah.

We each have many decisions and battles to fight each day. God knows the best way to fight our battles and approach our decisions. Like Jehoshaphat, we can insist on looking to Him first.

? Will you look to God and the words of His servants for guidance in your life?

Activity

Gather together some of the writings of the prophets. Have each person search and find something meaningful that a prophet has said. Invite everyone to share the counsel they found and how that counsel can direct our lives and decisions.

Book of 1 Kings

Elijah

Elijah was a prophet who mainly ministered and served among the people of the northern kingdom of Israel for many years after the two kingdoms split. He was called by God to help the people in Israel get rid of the wicked practices and habits their new queen, Jezebel, had brought into the country. She worshipped a false god named Baal, and when she married King Ahab, she persuaded him to build temples to Baal. These temples were used for wickedness. The Lord brought a drought upon the kingdom for three years to convince the king and queen to repent. Elijah was in hiding for the three years because Jezebel blamed him and wanted to kill him to bring back the rain. But the king and queen's guards could never find him. God performed many miracles through Elijah, including saving the starving widow of Zarephath and calling down fire from heaven on Mount Carmel. At the end of Elijah's life, a chariot of horses and fire took him away into heaven. The prophet Elisha picked up Elijah's cloak as it fell from the chariot, and he became the next prophet.

 Elijah lived during the times of King Ahab and Ahaziah. King Ahab is the king who united with King Jehoshaphat in battle.

 During Elijah's three years in hiding, the Lord sent ravens to deliver food to him. One of the places he hid was called Mount Horeb, which many people believe was also Mount Sinai, where Moses received the Ten Commandments.

 Elijah appeared with Moses to Peter, James, and John on the Mount of Transfiguration in New Testament times.

 Malachi, the last prophet of the Old Testament, prophesied that Elijah would return before the Savior's Second Coming.

 "And Elijah came unto all the people, and said, How long halt ye between two opinions? if the Lord be God, follow him" (1 Kings 18:21).

Anything, Anytime, Anywhere (1 Kings 18)

After hiding from Queen Jezebel and King Ahab for three years, Elijah came out of his caves and decided to show the people God's power once and for all. On top of Mount Carmel, 850 prophets of the false god Baal came to have a contest with Elijah. They laid out an altar with wood and decided that they would both call upon their god to send down fire from heaven and burn the altar. Whichever god did this would be recognized as the true and living God. The prophets of Baal went first. For hours they danced and whirled and did all sorts of crazy things around the altar to try to call down fire from heaven. Nothing happened. Finally, exhausted, they turned it over to Elijah. The great prophet tore down their altar and built a new one on twelve stones—each representing a tribe of Israel. Elijah poured twelve barrels of water over the altar and filled the trench surrounding it like a river. Then he prayed.

"The fire of the Lord fell, and consumed the burnt sacrifice, and the wood, and the stones, and the dust, and licked up the water that was in the trench." (1 Kings 18:38)

Elijah's God was the true God! Elijah then prayed again to the Lord and asked Him to send rain. For the first time in three years, black clouds gathered on Mount Carmel and the rains began to fall.

The God we love and worship is a mighty God. He can do anything, anytime, anywhere. Three years of drought or twelve barrels of water are not too much for the God of heaven and earth. He performed miracles for Elijah, and He can perform them for you.

? Will you choose to believe in a God of miracles—a God who can do anything, anytime, anywhere?

Activity

Make a list of miracles you remember from the Old and New Testaments. Ask everyone to draw or find a picture of their favorite miracle and take turns telling the story and why they love it. Hang the pictures up to remember the God of miracles.

The Widow of Zarephath

Book of 1 Kings

 The widow from the city of Zarephath was a woman who helped the prophet Elijah and witnessed some of his miracles. The prophet Elijah had to go into hiding after sealing the heavens, which he did because of the wickedness of the people led by King Ahab and Jezebel. Jezebel sent her guards all through the kingdom to look for and kill Elijah. One day, the Lord commanded Elijah to go to the city of Zarephath. He told Elijah a widow would take care of him there. The city of Zarephath was not in Israel, and the widow, most likely, would not have known all that Elijah knew about God and His prophets. Elijah met this widow on the day she was preparing her last small meal for her son and herself. The widow was very poor, and the famine had taken away all of her sources of food. Through an act of faith and a great miracle, the widow's food did not run out through the whole famine. Her son, however, caught an illness and died. But Elijah raised him from the dead, and the widow's faith in God and His power was strengthened.

 Zarephath was in the kingdom of Zidon, which is where Queen Jezebel was from.

 We do not know how old the widow and her son were. We also do not know whether she had any other children.

 Elijah most likely stayed with the widow through two or three years of the famine.

 Jesus Christ mentions the widow of Zarephath as an example of faith and God's goodness.

 "And the woman said to Elijah, Now by this I know that thou art a man of God, and that the word of the Lord in thy mouth is true" (1 Kings 17:24).

First Things First (1 Kings 17)

When Elijah first met the widow of Zarephath, she was carrying two sticks to make a fire to cook one last meal for herself and her son before they died. The famine had been very hard for their little family, and all that was left was enough to fill a little bit of their stomachs before death. Elijah asked the widow for some water as he saw her gathering her sticks. Without hesitation, the widow got a cup to fill with water for the friendly stranger. As she walked to get water, the prophet asked her for some bread. Sadly, the widow told him that all she had in her whole house was a handful of meal flour and a small amount of oil.

"And Elijah said unto her, Fear not; go and do as thou hast said: but make me thereof a little cake first, and bring it unto me, and after make for thee and for thy son." (1 Kings 17:13)

Elijah promised the widow if she would do as he asked, her flour barrel would never be empty and her oil cruse would never run out until the Lord sent rain again. Without any question, the widow prepared Elijah a cake of bread from her last bit of oil and flour. Just as Elijah had promised, the widow and her son were never hungry again.

It took a great amount of faith for the poor widow to put the prophet Elijah ahead of herself. It took greater faith for her to put the prophet ahead of her son. When we put God first in our lives, no matter our schedules or conditions or worries, He will always take care of us. His goodness will never fail.

? Will you put God first in your life? Will you schedule time for Him before anything else?

Activity

Make a chart of your activities every day. Graph out how much time is spent on work and school, relaxation, errands, friends, sleep, and also service and worship. Talk about and decide how you will make sure you are putting God first in your day.

Elisha

Book of 2 Kings

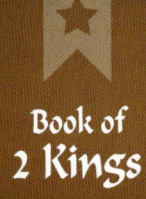 Elisha was a prophet who the Lord chose after He took Elijah into heaven. At the end of Elijah's life, Elisha watched Elijah split the Jordan River by slapping the water with his cloak. When Elijah was carried away by the chariot of fire into heaven, his cloak fell on Elisha as a symbol that he was to be the next prophet. Elisha took the cloak and slapped the water of the Jordan River, and it split before the people. They knew God had chosen him as the next prophet. Elisha continued the mission of Elijah to try to stop the wicked worship of Baal. Elisha spent most of his ministry in the northern kingdom of Israel. He performed many miracles of charity for the people of the kingdom, including the healing of a bitter spring of water, causing a lost axe head to float, and raising a boy from the dead. The kings of the northern kingdom of Israel looked to Elisha for advice and counsel. When Israel was in a war with Syria, Elisha revealed the plans of the Syrian army and assisted Israel's king and his armies in many battles.

 Elisha was a follower of Elijah, and they spent at least six years together before Elijah left.

 The ministry of Elisha lasted more than fifty years.

 The last miracle of Elisha's life happened after his death. When a dead person was put into the prophet's tomb, the person suddenly came back to life.

 Elisha was part of a group of believers and faithful followers of God known as "the sons of the prophets."

 "And when the sons of the prophets . . . saw him, they said, The spirit of Elijah doth rest on Elisha. And they came to meet him, and bowed themselves to the ground before him" (2 Kings 2:15).

They That Be With Us (2 Kings 6)

During the ministry of Elisha, the king of Syria, a neighboring enemy, attacked the kingdom of Israel. Every time the Syrians made plans, the Lord revealed them to Elisha, and then Elisha told them to the king of Israel. The Syrians were amazed at the secrets the Israelites knew, and the king wanted to find out how they did it. Someone in the Syrian camp knew about Elisha and told the king, so he sent an army to a place called Dothan to destroy Elisha. One morning, the servant of the prophet woke up early and found the city surrounded by hundreds of Syrian horses and chariots. He thought they were doomed and began to fear. Elisha was calm.

"And he answered, Fear not: for they that be with us are more than they that be with them." (2 Kings 6:16)

Elisha the prophet prayed that the servant's eyes could be opened spiritually. Suddenly the servant was shocked to see the mountains around them filled with chariots and horses of fire. God's army of angels had been there all along, even though the servant hadn't be able to see them. They were not alone, and the servant was no longer afraid.

Sometimes you may be discouraged by all the bad influences and wicked people in the world. You might be afraid and think good cannot win. In these moments, remember the story of Elisha and his servant. Remember whose side you are on—and who is on your side.

? In moments of doubt and fear, will you pray for eyes to see and a heart to feel the strength of God that surrounds you?

Activity

Memorize the scripture quoted in the story to the left (2 Kings 6:16). Carry it around on a notecard in your pocket for a few days to help you remember it. In moments of fear, recite the scripture to yourself or others to remember the strength that surrounds you.

Naaman

Book of 2 Kings

 During the time of Elisha the prophet, there was a great war between the northern kingdom of Israel and the country of Syria. One of the commanding generals of the Syrian army was a man named Naaman. Naaman was a man of great character and was a very strong military leader. He also suffered with the disease of leprosy. Naaman's wife had a servant girl who was from Israel, and one day she told Naaman's wife that in her home country there was a prophet who could perform miracles in the name of the Lord. The servant girl said he could heal Naaman. The general was excited and sent money, gifts, and a letter to the king of Israel asking to be healed, even though the two countries were at war with each other. Naaman went to the home of Elisha in Israel and asked for the miracle. He was miraculously healed of his disease and became a believer in God.

 In those times, no one knew of a cure for leprosy.

 Naaman returned home with two mounds of dirt from the land of Israel after his cleansing. He thought the dirt was special because it was from the country that worshipped the true God.

 Elisha would not receive any of the gifts Naaman tried to give him after he was healed. However, Elisha's servant, Gehazi, tried to take the gifts and was cursed with leprosy.

 Jesus spoke about Naaman and used him as an example to show God's goodness to non-Israelite people.

 "Naaman, captain of the host of the king of Syria, was a great man with his master, and honourable . . . he was also a mighty man in valour, but he was a leper" (2 Kings 5:1).

The Little Things (2 Kings 5)

Naaman traveled a long distance to stand at the door of Elisha the prophet to ask for a miracle. He was very disappointed when Elisha sent a servant out to talk with him instead of coming to see him face to face. Naaman was even more disappointed when the servant gave him Elisha's instructions to dip himself in the Jordan River seven times to be healed. The mighty war general expected that Elisha would come out and raise his hands high in the heaven and command him to be made whole. Instead, Elisha sent a servant to deliver instructions to go to the Jordan River—the dirty, slow-moving Jordan River! Syria had much better rivers! Naaman left in terrible, disappointed anger. As he and his servant walked away, his wise servant spoke up.

"If the prophet had bid thee do some great thing, wouldest thou not have done it? How much rather then, when he saith to thee, Wash, and be clean?" (2 Kings 5:13)

Naaman was humbled by his servant's faith and went to the Jordan River to dip himself in. After he came out of the water the seventh time, his body was as clean and new as a baby's. God had healed Naaman through a simple act of obedient faith.

Sometimes we might be like Naaman and expect to see grand signs and miracles from God. We might think we need to do big, expensive, and time-consuming things to show our belief in and love of God. Like Naaman, we need to learn that God reaches out to us through simple means. It is through simple things that we can show our love and appreciation to Him.

? Will you show a constant and simple love and devotion to God throughout your life?

Activity

Create a list of five simple things you can do this week to show your love and devotion to the Lord. Here are a few examples: One act of kindness. One prayer of praise. One small sacrifice. One word of encouragement. One moment of simple obedience.

Book of Jonah

Jonah

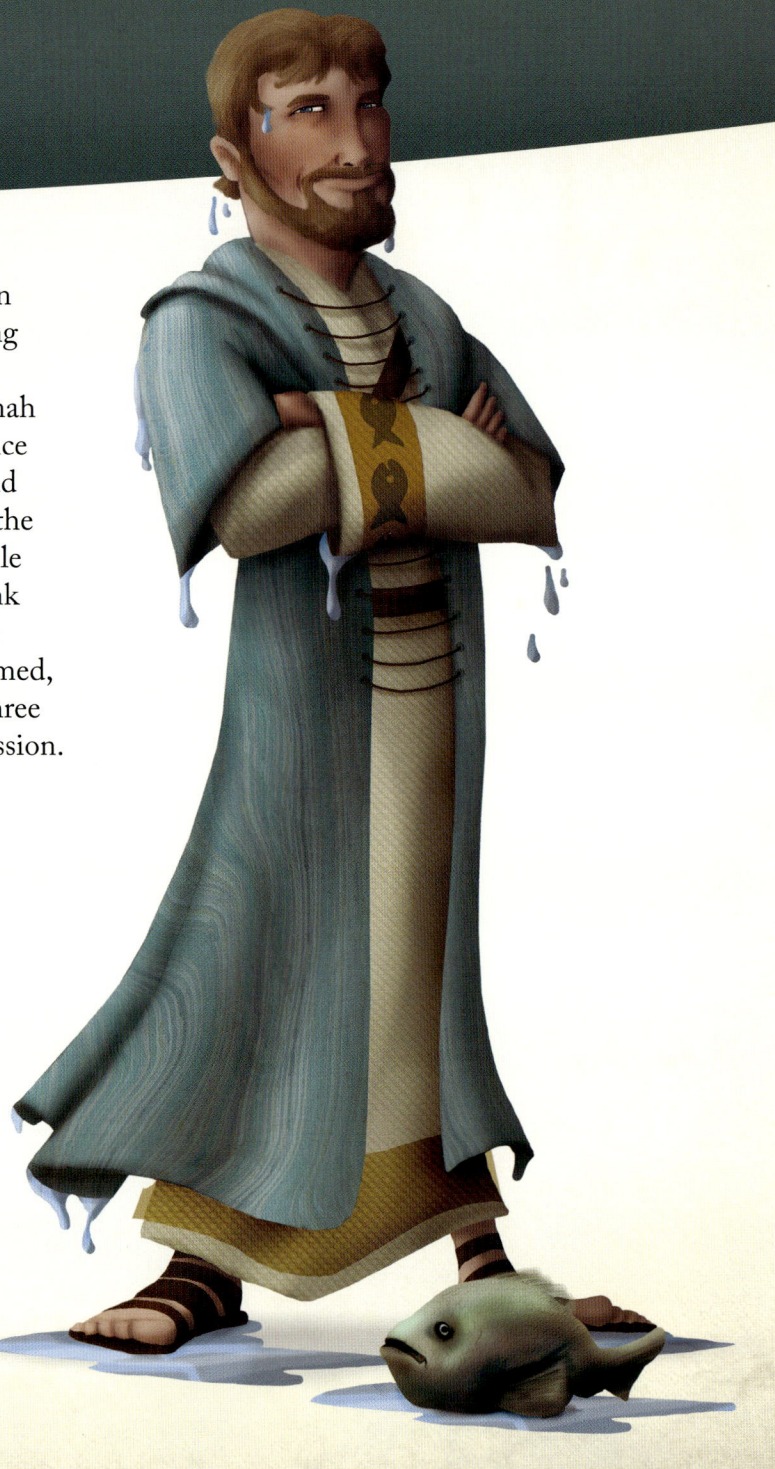

Jonah was a prophet of the Lord who ministered in the northern kingdom of Israel during the reign of King Jeroboam II. During this time, he prophesied that the kingdom would be expanded and become stronger during the king's reign—which it did. Jonah is most famous for his calling from the Lord to preach repentance to the city of Nineveh. The people of Nineveh were very wicked at the time, and the Lord wanted Jonah to help them change. Jonah was afraid of the city and the call, and he tried to flee in the opposite direction to a city called Tarshish. While Jonah was aboard a ship headed to Tarshish, a large storm came and nearly sunk the ship. Jonah knew the storm was sent by God because of his actions, and he asked his fellow sailors to throw him overboard. When they did, the storm calmed, but a large fish or whale swallowed Jonah. He was in the belly of the fish for three days before he was spit out. After that, he returned to Nineveh to fulfill his mission.

 Jonah was a prophet around the years 793 to 753 BC.

 Nineveh is the capital city of Assyria, an enemy of the kingdom of Israel. Assyria destroyed Israel, the northern kingdom, in about 722 BC.

 The people of Nineveh repented when Jonah taught them the gospel. Jonah was surprised by their change.

 Jesus compared His own burial and Resurrection to the story of Jonah (see Matthew 12:40).

 "Now the Lord had prepared a great fish to swallow up Jonah. And Jonah was in the belly of the fish three days and three nights" (Jonah 1:17).

A Second Time (Jonah 1–4)

Anyone would be scared of the city of Nineveh. The Assyrians were a wicked people and a cruel enemy of the kingdom of Israel. Perhaps Jonah thought they would kill him. Perhaps he did not think they deserved to hear the message of forgiveness from God. Whatever the reason, Jonah tried to run away from God. He was fast asleep down inside the ship when the captain came to wake him up in desperate need of help. Jonah had slept through a storm so violent the ship was about to break in half. The sailors had tried to outrun the storm. They had paddled hard and thrown their gear overboard, but it was no use. Jonah knew the storm was sent from the Lord. He asked the crewmen to throw him overboard. They threw Jonah into the wild sea. As he kicked his legs to stay afloat, a giant fish came from the depths of the ocean and swallowed Jonah in one gulp. He spent three days in the belly of the fish. After Jonah's prayer for forgiveness, the Lord spoke to the fish and it spit him out.

"And the word of the Lord came unto Jonah the second time, saying, Arise, go unto Nineveh." (Jonah 3:1–2)

Even the wicked city of Nineveh deserved another chance to hear the message about God's forgiveness and love. Jonah learned that from a few days inside a fish. Instead of leaving Jonah to drown in the sea, God prepared a giant fish to save Jonah and give him a chance to try again.

The worth of every soul is great to God. He sent His Son to the world to die for all. The Savior spent three days in the belly of the earth and came forth alive again in order to give everyone like Jonah and the people of Nineveh a chance to try a second time.

? When you or someone else you know makes a mistake, will you accept God's forgiveness and try again?

Activity

Put drops of food coloring into a clear pitcher or vase of water. Then pour in bleach until the water clears. Read Isaiah 1:18 and talk about how Christ can clear our sins and let us try again.

Book of Daniel
Daniel

 Around the year 600 BC, the nation of Judah was taken over by the Babylonians and many of the Jews were taken to Babylon as slaves. Daniel was a young man at this time and was one of the exiles. The Babylonian king, Nebuchadnezzar, brought Daniel into the royal courts to train him to be a government leader. Most likely, Daniel was from the royal family in Jerusalem. He was raised and trained for three years in the Babylonian courts—learning the ways of the government, language, and culture. Daniel showed great courage when he refused to eat the king's meats, which were forbidden by the Lord at that time. The Lord gave Daniel the gift to interpret dreams because of his faithfulness. Daniel interpreted the dreams of Nebuchadnezzar, and on one occasion he saved the lives of many people. He lived in Babylon his entire life as a leader in the government. Toward the end of his life, he was one of the three presidents during the reign of King Darius. Daniel is most famous for the time he was thrown into the lions' den and came out unharmed.

 Daniel was given a new Babylonian name when he was taken there. It was Belteshazzar.

 Most Bible scholars think Daniel was a teenager when he was taken to Babylon.

 Daniel went to Babylon to be trained with his three friends, Hananiah, Mishael, and Azariah, who were later named Shadrach, Meshach, and Abed-nego.

 King Nebuchadnezzar was a Babylonian king, but King Darius was a Persian king who was appointed over the area of the Babylonian capital after the Persians conquered Babylon.

 "The king answered unto Daniel, and said, Of a truth it is, that your God is a God of gods, and a Lord of kings, and a revealer of secrets, seeing thou couldest reveal this secret. Then the king made Daniel a great man" (Daniel 2:47–48).

An Open Window (Daniel 6)

King Darius learned to love and trust Daniel very much. When the king appointed three presidents to help him rule over the people, he selected Daniel to be the head of the three. Daniel had the gift of wisdom and great leadership skills that made the life of the king much easier. However, the other officials in the government grew jealous of Daniel's success. One day they tricked the king into signing a law that made it illegal for anyone to pray for thirty days. Anyone who broke the law would be thrown into a den of lions to be eaten.

"Now when Daniel knew that the writing was signed, he went into his house; and his windows being open in his chamber toward Jerusalem, he kneeled upon his knees three times a day, and prayed." (Daniel 6:10)

The great prophet Daniel made it no secret that he was going to pray to God whether there was a law against it or not. The enemies of Daniel forced the king to follow the law he had signed, and Daniel was thrown into the lions' den. Through the night, the Lord sent an angel to close the mouths of the lions and protect Daniel. The king was elated when he learned the Lord had saved Daniel.

Daniel was not afraid of living according to his faith. He did not care what other people thought about him or his relationship with God. He loved the Lord and was going to obey Him no matter what—with his window wide open.

You may sometimes feel weird or different for loving God and choosing to follow Him. Each of us can be like Daniel and show our love and devotion to God without any embarrassment or shame.

? Will you be an example of your faith and not be afraid to show your belief in and love of God?

Activity

Find a way as a family to publicly declare something you believe in. A good way to do this may be to post or share something on a social network that shows your love for and belief in God.

Shadrach, Meshach, Abed-nego

Book of Daniel

 These three friends came into Babylon as prisoners when Jerusalem was taken over by King Nebuchadnezzar. Shadrach, Meshach, and Abed-nego were exiles with Daniel the prophet and were most likely close to the same age. They, like Daniel, were trained in Nebuchadnezzar's court to become officials in the Babylonian government. Their names were changed to Shadrach, Meshach, and Abed-nego (Babylonian names) when they were taken into captivity. The three friends stood with Daniel and refused to eat the foods the king gave them, which the Lord had forbidden at the time. Eventually, the king made the three friends officials in his kingdom. While they were serving as officials, the king made a new law that everyone had to bow down and worship a large statue he had made. Shadrach, Meshach, and Abed-nego refused and were thrown into the king's fiery furnace, but God saved them.

 Their Hebrew names were Hananiah, Mishael, and Azariah, which were names that reflected faith in God. Their names were changed to fit Babylonian custom.

 These boys were most likely from a royal family in Jerusalem and most likely came to Babylon as teenagers.

 During different times of the Old Testament, the Lord commanded His people to not eat certain meats, such as pig and certain seafood.

 King Nebudchadnezzar originally gave a high government position only to Daniel, but Daniel convinced the king to make Shadrach, Meshach, and Abed-nego rulers as well.

 "As for these four children, God gave them knowledge and skill in all learning and wisdom" (Daniel 1:17).

But If Not (Daniel 3)

One day, King Nebuchadnezzar decided to make a giant statue of gold and set it up in his kingdom. He hired some musicians and made a law that whenever the music played, all were required to bow down to the golden statue. Shadrach, Meshach, and Abed-nego had made promises with God that they would not bow down and worship any other person or thing besides Him. When jealous and angry officials saw that the three young men would not bow down to the statue, they took them before the king. King Nebuchadnezzar was furious! He demanded that they obey him and bow down or he would throw them into a fiery furnace. The boys stayed true to God.

"If it be so, our God whom we serve is able to deliver us from the burning fiery furnace, and he will deliver us . . . but if not, be it known . . . we will not serve thy gods." (Daniel 3:17–18)

Shadrach, Meshach, and Abed-nego knew that God had the power to save them from the fire of the furnace—even when the king turned up the heat seven times hotter than normal. However, even if God decided He would not save them—though He could—they still would not disobey. No matter what! The king ordered the boys to be thrown in the furnace. To the king's amazement, when he looked into the flames, he saw four figures inside instead of three. The fourth looked like the Son of God. The king quickly pulled the boys out and promised to never disrespect their God again.

Our God is mighty and powerful. Sometimes He stops bad things from happening, and sometimes He does not. Whichever He decides in your life, you can be sure He will always stand beside you.

? Will you be courageous and always stand up for what is right no matter the consequences?

Activity

Make a list of some of the commandments that God has given to us. Under each one, list some of the worldly opposition and heavenly blessings that could come from obeying the commandments. Decide together that even if we face opposition, we will all still be faithful and true.

Book of Esther
Esther, Queen of Persia

Queen Esther was a humble Jewish girl who became a powerful Persian queen and saved her people. When Persia conquered Babylon, all of the Jews who had been living as slaves and exiles in Babylon were allowed to return home. Many of the Jews did not return to Jerusalem, but stayed to live in the new Persian empire. Esther was one of those. She was raised by her older cousin Mordecai. One day, the Persian king Ahasuerus ordered all of the unmarried women to come to the palace so he could pick a new bride to be queen. After a year of preparation and waiting, the women were presented to the king, and he picked Esther as the new queen. One of the king's officers, Haman, did not like the Jews and tricked the king into signing a death order for all Jews living in the kingdom. The king and Haman did not know Esther was a Jew. Esther showed great courage and confronted the king to plead for her people and tell him the truth about her religion. Against Haman's hopes and plans, the people of God were saved. Because of Esther, they remained free to believe and worship however they wanted.

 Esther's Hebrew name was Hadassah. She was most likely given her new Persian name, Esther, by the king's people when she moved into the palace.

 Mordecai, Esther's uncle, worked at the palace and offended Haman, the king's officer, by not bowing down to him. This is why Haman arranged the killing of the Jews.

 Ahasuerus chose Esther as his queen around the year 478 BC.

 Esther was an orphan from the tribe of Benjamin.

 "Go, gather together all the Jews that are present . . . and fast ye for me . . . I also and my maidens will fast likewise; and so will I go in unto the king, which is not according to the law: and if I perish, I perish" (Esther 4:16).

For Such a Time as This (Esther 1–5)

Queen Esther was terrified when the lives of all of her people rested on her shoulders. She wanted to talk to the king, but she had not seen him for many days. No one, not even the queen, was allowed to approach the king uninvited. The penalty for doing so was death. As Esther prayed and worried about what might happen to her people, the day of decision was getting closer. What would she do? Her cousin Mordecai wrote her a letter and reminded her how many people's lives were in danger if she did not risk her life to go before the king. Mordecai also encouraged and comforted her by reminding her that God knew all things and perhaps put her in this position for a reason.

"Who knoweth whether thou art come to the kingdom for such a time as this?" (Esther 4:14)

Mordecai's letter gave Esther great courage. She wrote back and asked her cousin to gather all of the believers together and to fast for her for three days. Esther gathered all of her maidens in the palace, and they fasted as well. Together, they pleaded with the Lord for a miracle. And a miracle they received! Esther's heart was afire with bravery, and the king's heart was softened when he saw her enter the throne room. The people were saved!

God has put each of us in certain places at certain times to do great things. Sometimes we forget that and need reminders and encouragement to do hard things. Great strength can come to someone when many are gathered together in common faith and prayer.

? Will you surround yourself with people who will remind you of your potential and who will gather with you in doing good?

Activity

Organize a service project or acts of goodness you can do as a family. Perhaps there is another family who needs your prayers or help. Invite others to either pray or participate with you, and watch for the miracles that come as a group unites in a good cause.

Book of Job

Job

Job is one of the most pitied and also most admired people in the Bible. His patience and endurance during difficult trials are famous. Job was a wealthy landowner. He had a wife, seven sons, three daughters, 7,000 sheep, 3,000 camels, 500 yoke of oxen, 500 donkeys, and a magnificent house. Job was a righteous man and hated evil. He was considered by his friends and neighbors to be one of the greatest men they knew. One day, servant after servant came to Job with bad news. All of his animals had died in different disasters. The last servant brought the worst news of all: a great wind had knocked over the house where his children were eating, and they had all died. Soon after this, Job got boils all over his body and was itchy and stinky. At first his friends felt bad for him, but eventually they abandoned him. His wife urged him to turn against God for what He was doing to Job. Job refused this advice and stayed faithful to God his whole life. At the end, God blessed Job with twice as much as he had possessed before.

 The Book of Job is written as a Hebrew poem. Many people consider it to be the most beautifully written book in the Bible.

 We do not know exactly when Job lived. Different Bible scholars guess anywhere from before Noah's flood to the time of Moses. That is a span of 1,000 years!

 Boils are open sores that people can get on their skin. Job had boils from the top of his head to the bottom of his feet and would scratch them with broken pottery.

 Job lived 140 years and was able to meet three generations of grandchildren.

 "Though he slay me, yet will I trust in him: but I will maintain mine own ways before him" (Job 13:15).

Happy Endings (Job 1–42)

A few days after Job lost everything in his life, three of his friends came to visit him. They had heard about the awful things that happened and came to give their comfort and advice. They sat and cried with him for seven days. As more time passed and things did not get better, Job's friends began to wonder why everything bad was happening to him. They told him he was being punished because he was a sinful man. Job had a greater understanding and stayed faithful to the Lord through extremely difficult trials. He was not sure why these things were happening, but he knew God had not abandoned him. After a long time of suffering and hardship, Job testified that he had both heard and seen the Lord. He was greatly blessed.

"So the Lord blessed the latter end of Job more than his beginning." (Job 42:12)

Job ended his life with 14,000 sheep, 6,000 camels, 1,000 yoke of oxen, 1,000 donkeys, seven sons, and three beautiful daughters. Although he wondered during the hard years why he was having such a difficult life, he always knew God was there, and he never turned his back on the Lord.

Bad things happen to good people. Most of the time we do not know why these things happen. Just because we suffer in mortal life does not mean God is angry or has abandoned us. If we stay patient and true to God during those times, we, like Job, will be able to witness that we have seen the hand of the Lord during even our hardest days.

? Will you stay faithful and true during life's hardest times? Will you look for the Lord during your darkest days?

Activity

Visit a building or other structure that is lit up at nighttime, or spend an evening under the stars. Talk about how these things shine more beautifully when it is dark. Discuss how we can still see the hand of God during our dark times and how He can give us strength.

The Four Gospels

Mary & Joseph

 Mary and Joseph were among the most faithful disciples of Jesus Christ. These two mighty souls were given the responsibility to care for, teach, and raise the Son of God from the time He was a baby. Mary first learned she would be given this blessed responsibility when she was a young woman living in the poor town of Nazareth. The angel Gabriel appeared to her and announced that she would be the mother of Jesus, the Savior. Soon after, an angel appeared to Joseph and told him to marry his betrothed Mary, who would bear the Son of God. The angel told both of them the baby's name would be Jesus. Joseph and Mary went to Bethlehem to pay taxes, and while they were there, Jesus was born and then laid in a manger. The king, Herod, had heard that Jesus would be called King of the Jews. Herod grew jealous and made plans to kill the baby Jesus. Mary and Joseph were warned by an angel to flee into Egypt. After Herod died, the family returned to their hometown of Nazareth to raise their son. Mary brought Jesus into the world and she was at the foot of the cross when He was crucified. She was the only person who was with Jesus throughout His entire life and ministry.

 The parents of Jesus, according to historical custom, would have been in their teenage years when Jesus was born.

 Mary and Joseph were from the tribe of Judah. The Lord promised Abraham that the Savior would come through his family line. Judah was Abraham's great-grandson.

 Many people believe Joseph died sometime between when Jesus was twelve and the beginning of His ministry, since he is not mentioned again in the Gospels.

 Mary and Joseph were also the parents of four other sons and some daughters.

 "And the angel came in unto her, and said, Hail, thou that art highly favoured, the Lord is with thee: blessed art thou among women" (Luke 1:28).

Behold the Handmaid (Luke 1–2)

The angel Gabriel must have startled Mary when he appeared to her unexpectedly. She was engaged to be married to Joseph, the carpenter, and they were probably beginning to plan their home and life together. Neither of them likely knew what the Lord was about to ask them to do. They knew the scriptures and knew the prophecies of a Savior who would come to save them from their sins. They did not know, however, that they would raise Him. The angelic visits came with a promise that nothing was impossible with God. It was a promise Mary and Joseph probably held on to. Mary delivered her first baby in a stable and laid him in a trough used for hay. The king hunted them. They lived as refugees and exiles in a foreign and unknown country. There were miracles and there were dangers. There were sweet,tender moments, and terrifying nights. In the end, Mary found herself at the foot of the cross with bitter tears on her cheeks. Mary and Joseph did not live normal lives. Their sacred calling required something more than ordinary. We do not know how much Mary anticipated or knew at the beginning, but her response to the angel revealed her heart:

"Behold the handmaid of the Lord; be it unto me according to thy word." (Luke 1:38)

In other words, "My life is in His hands. I am ready." Joseph answered in a similar way. They were both ready and willing to do whatever the Lord asked them to do—committed to the very end.

? Are you willing to hand your heart and life over to Jesus? Are you available and willing and committed from birth until death?

Activity

Look through some family picture albums. Talk about some of the unexpected turns and challenges you have faced. Share the moments you decided to be available, willing, and committed no matter what life brought.

Zacharias & Elisabeth

The Four Gospels

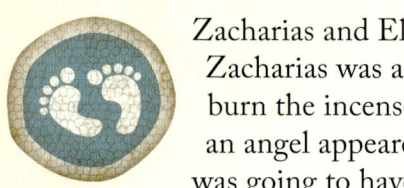 Zacharias and Elisabeth were the faithful parents of John the Baptist. Zacharias was a priest for the temple. One day he was chosen to burn the incense in the holy place inside. While he was there, an angel appeared to him to tell him that his wife, Elisabeth, was going to have a son who would prepare the people for the coming of the Savior. When Zacharias doubted, he became mute as a sign to show that the angel had told the truth. When Elisabeth was about six months into her pregnancy, her cousin Mary came to visit her with the news that she would have a miraculous baby as well. Elisabeth's baby jumped inside her when she heard Mary's greeting. She knew about Jesus before Mary ever told her. When Elisabeth's baby was born, family and friends wanted to name the baby Zacharias, but Zacharias wrote down on a tablet that the baby's name was John. When he did that, the Lord allowed Zacharias to speak again, and he prophesied about his son's mission and the mission of Jesus Christ. Zacharias and Elisabeth lived in the beautiful Judean hillside near Jerusalem.

 Elisabeth had been called barren, meaning she could not have children. She was very old when she had John the Baptist, who was her only child.

 Zacharias and Elisabeth were both from the tribe of Levi. Only members of the tribe of Levi were allowed to serve in the temple.

 The responsibility to burn incense in the temple was a great honor that was determined by casting lots. Usually a priest only received the privilege once in his life.

 The Bible calls Elisabeth and Mary cousins. People disagree whether that means first cousins or some other family relationship. Either way, their relationship made Jesus and John the Baptist relatives as well.

 "And they were both righteous before God, walking in all the commandments and ordinances of the Lord blameless" (Luke 1:6).

Waiting (Luke 1)

In Bible times, when a woman could not have any children, it was often considered to be a curse. Naturally, this made barren women very sad and upset. Many people looked down upon a woman who could not have a baby. Despite what others may have said or how they treated her, Elisabeth was faithful and obedient to the Lord her whole life. So was her husband, Zacharias. For many years, the couple prayed to God that He would bless them with a child. As time passed, they may have thought that God had not heard their prayers or had decided not to answer them. When the angel Gabriel announced to Zacharias that he was going to be a father, he could not believe it. He was shocked! It was impossible!

"Fear not, Zacharias: for thy prayer is heard." (Luke 1:13)

Even though Zacharias was old and his wife was barren, the Lord was going to bless them with a baby boy. And not just any baby boy—a prophet who was called to prepare the world for the coming of Jesus Christ.

Perhaps Elisabeth and Zacharias had already given up on their dreams and prayers of having a child. Waiting can be so hard. Sometimes it can cause someone to turn away from the Lord out of anger or bitterness. But not Zacharias and Elisabeth.

Sometimes God answers prayers quickly. Sometimes God answers prayers slowly. Sometimes God doesn't answer prayers the way we expected He would. If we wait patiently and faithfully on the Lord, eventually—perhaps not until heaven—God will grant us the righteous gifts we seek.

? Will you wait patiently on the Lord for your blessings? Will you stay faithful even when your prayers seem unanswered?

Activity

Plant different types of seeds in cups or small planters. Water them and place them by the window for light. Teach that all seeds require patience. During the weeks ahead, as each plant blooms and grows at different rates, talk about how God answers prayers in different ways and at different times.

The Four Gospels

John the Baptist

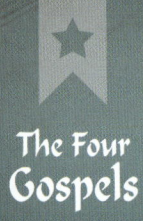

John the Baptist was the only son of the faithful Elisabeth and Zacharias and was chosen to be the forerunner for the Savior, preparing the way for His mortal ministry. John's mother, Elisabeth, and Jesus's mother, Mary, were cousins and were pregnant at the same time. John was born about six months before Jesus. The Bible tells us that John grew up in the wilderness and lived off the land. When he was older, John began to preach repentance to people in the wilderness and to baptize them. He had many followers who came to hear his teachings. Jesus Christ came to John the Baptist when he was teaching near a river and asked to be baptized. Even though John felt unworthy, he baptized Jesus in the Jordan River. Soon after, Jesus began His public ministry. John continued to teach people about the Savior and lead people to Him his whole life. John offended the wife of King Herod, Herodias, when he told her she was living a wicked life. She tricked her husband into killing John the Baptist, which caused great sadness in the Church.

 One of the followers of John the Baptist was Andrew, the brother of the apostle Peter.

 John baptized Jesus at a place in the Jordan River called Bethabara. It is near the Dead Sea and is one of the lowest places on earth.

 The wilderness where John lived and preached was the same wilderness where Moses and the children of Israel wandered and the same one where Elijah hid from Ahab and Jezebel.

 John the Baptist died in the prison of Herod in about 32 AD.

 "Verily I say unto you, Among them that are born of women there hath not risen a greater than John the Baptist: notwithstanding he that is least in the kingdom of heaven is greater than he" (Matthew 11:11).

Prepare the Way (Matthew 3)

John the Baptist must have been an interesting sight. He grew up and lived in the wilderness of Judea for many, many years before the baptism of Jesus Christ. Perhaps he smelled a little funny. Maybe his hair was a little long and wild. He might have dressed in a tunic or robe made of matted and scratchy camel hair. When he was hungry, he found wild honey and locusts and other bugs to eat. But when he taught, he taught with power and a convincing spirit. Many people came to hear about the coming of the Lord in the near future. His mission was given to him before he was ever born:

"Prepare ye the way of the Lord, make his paths straight." (Matthew 3:3)

When a king visited an ancient city, a group of servants always went in front of him on the road. Their job was to make the road as smooth and straight as possible for the coming king. That was John's mission for the true King. John was surprised when Jesus came to the banks of the river where John was teaching and asked to be baptized. John resisted. John did not even feel worthy to unbuckle the sandals of the greatest man who would ever live. Jesus reassured him and expressed His love and confidence. John baptized Jesus and continued his mission of preparing the road in front of the Savior.

You might not feel you are a good choice to do the Lord's work. You might think He needs someone smarter, or richer, or more talented. But like John, no matter our family or home or possessions, we can help other people to know and believe in Jesus Christ. We can prepare the road for when He comes again.

? Will you help prepare the people you know for the coming of the Savior? Will you help them to know and love Him now?

Activity

Prepare a nice dinner with fancy plates and place settings. Have everyone help clean the house and prepare it as if an honored guest were coming. When you sit down to eat, talk about things you can do to best prepare yourselves and others for when Jesus comes again.

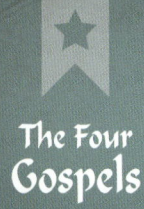

The Four Gospels

Peter

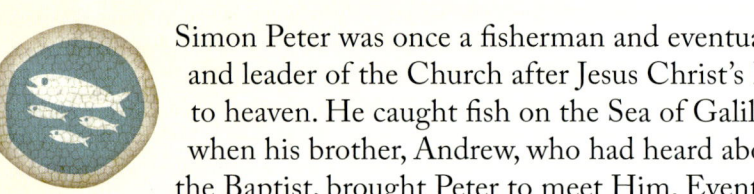
Simon Peter was once a fisherman and eventually became the chief apostle and leader of the Church after Jesus Christ's Resurrection and return to heaven. He caught fish on the Sea of Galilee. He first met Jesus when his brother, Andrew, who had heard about Jesus from John the Baptist, brought Peter to meet Him. Eventually, Jesus asked Peter to leave his fishing boats behind and become His disciple full time—teaching and preaching the gospel message to everyone he met. Peter was able to witness many miracles and develop a close relationship with the Lord during His three years of ministry. The night Jesus was arrested, Peter challenged the soldiers of the high priest and cut off their leader's ear. Jesus stopped him. Peter followed Jesus and His captors into the palace of Caiaphus, where Jesus was held in prison and put on trial. That night, Peter denied Jesus three times. Despite his mistakes and weaknesses, Peter became a wonderful leader of the Christians. He looked to God to help him during times of great persecution as the Church expanded through Europe and Asia.

 Peter's name was originally Simon. Jesus called him Peter when He met him. It means "the rock."

 After the Resurrection, Jesus Christ appeared to Peter by himself and then at least twice more to Peter and the other Apostles. They were witnesses of His Resurrection.

 Peter was one of twelve faithful followers of Christ who were called as the twelve disciples or Twelve Apostles. They had a special ministry to perform in this calling.

 Tradition says that Peter was killed for his belief in Christ and was crucified upside down.

 "And Simon Peter answered and said, Thou art the Christ, the Son of the living God. And Jesus answered and said unto him, Blessed art thou, Simon Bar-jona: for flesh and blood hath not revealed it unto thee, but my Father which is in heaven" (Matthew 16:16–17).

Reach (Matthew 14)

Peter may have thought the greatest thing he was ever going to do in his life was to become an expert fisherman, but the Lord saw something greater in Peter and wanted him to see it, too. One night, the disciples were out on a ship on the sea. The winds were blowing wildly, and for many hours the men in the boat worried, and rowed, and prayed for help. Late in the night or in the early morning, they saw a figure walking toward them. Soon they realized it was Jesus—walking on water! Peter grabbed the edge of the rocking ship and asked the Lord to call him out on the water.

"And He said, Come. And when Peter was come down out of the ship, he walked on the water, to go to Jesus." (Matthew 14:29)

Peter had spent his whole life working on the water, but never walking on the water.

As he walked closer to Jesus, the waves got bigger and the wind howled louder. Peter started to fear and then began to sink. He cried and reached for help! Immediately, Jesus stretched out His hand and caught him. Together, they walked back to the ship.

Peter continued to accomplish wonderful things the rest of his life. The Lord helped him understand an important lesson for all of us: He will ask us to do incredible things—incredible and frightening things. They will require us to "step out of the boat," face fears, and reach and stretch for the Lord. He will be there. He will not let us sink. He will show us how to do incredible things.

? Will you reach and stretch for the Lord? Will you let him show you the great things you are capable of?

Activity

Put a sticker high on a wall or on the ceiling out of reach. Have everyone try to touch it on their own. Then lift them just high enough that they can touch it if they reach. Talk about how this relates to the work we do for the Lord. How does He help us stretch? Where is He as we are reaching?

The Four Gospels

The Woman at the Well

The Bible does not give us her name, but in the Gospel of John we read the story of a woman who Jesus met when He stopped to rest at a well. When the Lord and His disciples were traveling to Galilee, they crossed through another country called Samaria. Jesus's disciples went into the city to get some food while He rested by a well. A certain woman came to the well to draw water and met the Lord there. Jesus asked her if she would get Him a drink. This surprised her, since Jesus was a Jew. In those times, those from Judea did not talk with people from Samaria. Through the conversation, Jesus told the woman things He knew about her even though they were strangers. Eventually, He told her that He was the Savior. The woman was so happy to meet and talk with Him. She was so excited to tell the people of the city that she left her water pot behind at the well and hurried to tell everyone she could about Jesus.

-  Jesus and the woman met at a well that is called Jacob's Well. It was in a place where Jacob (or Israel) once lived in Old Testament times and built a well for his family.

- During Old Testament times, this well was near the capital of the northern kingdom of Israel. Many Assyrians came to live there during the invasion and mixed with the Israelites who lived there—this is why the Jews did not like them.

- Jesus stayed in Samaria for two days after His conversation with the woman.

- The woman at the well had been married five times before meeting Jesus. She was very surprised when Jesus knew this about her.

- *"And many of the Samaritans of that city believed on him for the saying of the woman, which testified, He told me all that ever I did"* (John 4:39).

Routine and Ordinary (John 4)

The woman at the well was very surprised when the man from Judea talked to her. She did not know who He was, and she did not know what was about to happen. She came to the well that day, like she did every other day, to fetch water for her cooking, cleaning, drinking, and bathing. It was just a normal day in Samaria for her. When Jesus asked her for a drink, she reminded Him that she was a Samaritan and He was a Jew.

"Jesus answered . . . If thou knewest the gift of God and who it is that saith to thee, Give me to drink; thou wouldest have asked of him, and he would have given thee living water." (John 4:10)

The woman was confused by His answer, but continued to talk to Him as she drew water for herself and for the stranger. Slowly, through the conversation, the Lord helped her realize who He was. She had heard about the Messiah who was going to come. When she learned that this man was the Messiah, she ran into the city and convinced many others to come and find out for themselves. She probably never imagined that she would have such a beautiful, spiritual experience at such a simple, normal place. A conversation at the well changed her life forever.

The woman at the well learned that special, sacred moments can happen in ordinary places on ordinary days. Anyone can open the scriptures to read the Lord's words and speak to Him in prayer at any place and at any time. Those simple encounters with Him can change our day and our life.

? Will you read His words and talk with Him in your ordinary places and on your ordinary days?

Activity

Get a small copy of the Bible for each person to carry around for the whole week. Ask everyone to find a time or two each day that they can stop during their regular routine and have their own "moment at the well" reading the scriptures. (Young children can find time with their parents throughout the day.) Talk about these experiences together at the end of the week.

The Four Gospels

The One Leper

Jesus healed many people during His ministry and life on the earth. Everywhere He went, people would stop Him, tell Him about their problems, and look to Him for healing and miracles. One day as He was traveling to Jerusalem, He passed through Samaria and Galilee. As He entered into a village, he saw ten lepers who were standing far off. Lepers were not allowed to live within the walls of the city. Their disease, leprosy, was considered dangerous and contagious. They called to Jesus from a distance and begged Him for mercy. These ten people had heard about Him before He ever came to their village, and they knew He could help them. When Jesus sent them to see the priest, they were cleansed from leprosy as they walked away. Excited, nine of them ran home. One of them turned back and thanked Jesus for the miracle.

 Leprosy is a painful skin disease. It causes sores on your skin and sometimes makes parts of your skin and body fall off. Many people died from it.

 Lepers were required by law to yell "Unclean!" whenever someone was coming near them. Sometimes they were required to carry a bell to ring as a warning as well.

 People with leprosy were not allowed to serve in the temple or worship in public places until they had been pronounced clean by a priest.

 We don't know how many of the lepers might have been Samaritans, but we know that at least the one who returned was.

 "There met him ten men that were lepers, which stood afar off: And they lifted up their voices, and said, Jesus, Master, have mercy on us" (Luke 17:12–13).

Turn Back (Luke 17)

It is hard to imagine how sad the life of a leper must have been. Once people got the disease, their entire life changed. They could not live with their friends or family, could not worship, and could not hug, shake hands, or be near any other people. They were very lonely as they waited for their lives to slowly and painfully end. It was a terrible fate. When the ten lepers heard about Jesus coming to their village, they all called to Him, hoping for mercy. Jesus's instructions were simple enough. All they needed to do was go see their priest. As they went together, they were all cleansed. They were free from the horrible life they were living. Jesus had saved them from their sadness.

"And one of them, when he saw that he was healed, turned back, and with a loud voice glorified God." (Luke 17:15)

Jesus asked his new thankful friend where the other nine lepers were that were cleansed, but none of them could be found. He praised the leper for his faith and sent him happily home. All ten lepers were healed of their leprosy, but nine of them went home without expressing gratitude.

In our day, it can be a rare thing to find a thankful person. People who recognize the goodness and grace of others are a treasure. Perhaps they are even one in ten. The one leper's thankful heart led to a personal, powerful experience with Jesus. Gratitude is one of the greatest virtues.

? Will you be like the one leper and always remember to turn back and thank others—especially God? Will you express gratitude for both the little things and big things?

Activity

Try offering a prayer of pure thanksgiving. Do not ask for anything. Set a time and try to pray for at least a full minute expressing only gratitude. Can you do it for five minutes? ten?

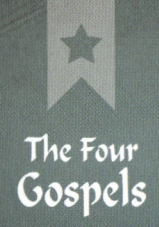

The Four Gospels

The Widow Who Gave Two Mites

During the last week of His mortal life and ministry, Jesus spent many hours teaching in the temple. Some of His most famous lessons and parables were given during these last days inside the temple walls. During one of those days, Jesus was with His disciples when a widow came into the treasury, the part of the temple where people came to donate money to help with the work of the temple. In the treasury area, there were thirteen trumpet-shaped boxes for people to put their money in. Many people were putting in large amounts of money, but the widow put in two mites, which was not very much. Jesus taught His disciples that the widow gave more than the others who were putting in great riches. She gave all that she had, while the others gave only a small part. Jesus praised her and used her as an example of sacrifice and faith.

 In Bible times, a widow could not own property, and usually the only way she made money was by either begging for it or getting the leftover scraps from others.

 A mite was the least valuable coin in Judea. Some Bible scholars estimate it was worth about six minutes of an average daily wage.

 The area of the temple with the treasury was called the "Court of the Women." Only covenant Israelites were allowed in this section.

 Herod's temple complex was huge. Some Bible scholars think it was about thirty acres. That is as big as nearly thirty football fields!

 "Of a truth I say unto you, that this poor widow hath cast in more than they all: For all these have of their abundance cast in unto the offerings of God: but she of her penury hath cast in all the living that she had" (Luke 21:3–4).

Noticed (Mark 12)

The last week of Jesus's life was also the week when the people celebrated the Passover. This was a feast and holy celebration to remember when the Lord delivered their people from bondage in Egypt. Thousands of people had gathered in Jerusalem for the Passover. The city was packed. The temple was crowded. Many languages were being spoken, money was being exchanged, sacrifices were being offered, families were preparing, old friends were meeting, and people were loud and busy. The temple was an easy place to blend in and be overlooked. In the treasury, people were giving their offerings and gifts. The clanging of the coins added to the background noise when the small, poor widow walked into the temple. She wouldn't have had fancy clothes or anything to make her stand out. Probably no one even noticed she was there—not even Jesus's disciples. But He did.

"And he called unto him his disciples." (Mark 12:43)

Jesus noticed her. He knew how poor she was and that those were her last coins. He knew the depth of her sacrifice, and He knew her heart.

You might feel overlooked by others. In fact, you probably sometimes are. Many times, even Jesus's closest disciples will not notice the good you do, the sacrifices you make, and the hard times you face. But He does. Jesus notices. And He knows your heart, too.

> **?** Will you continue to quietly and deliberately live a good life—even if, and perhaps especially when, no one else notices?

Activity

Decide on and carry out a secret act of service for someone—it can be a friend or a complete stranger!

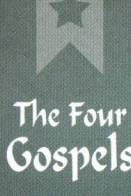

The Four Gospels

Mary & Martha

 Many people followed, loved, and helped the Lord during His life and ministry. Among these people were many faithful women, including Mary and Martha. These two wonderful sisters lived in a beautiful city called Bethany on the eastern side of the Mount of Olives. Bethany was a favorite place for the Savior to go and spend time—perhaps in part because of these faithful sisters. Martha and Mary were sisters of Lazarus, another friend and disciple of Jesus Christ. Toward the end of the Lord's ministry, Lazarus became sick and died. The sisters sent messages to Jesus to come, but He didn't arrive until Lazarus had been dead for a few days. The sisters were sure that if Jesus had come sooner, their brother would not have died. But they knew that whatever Jesus asked of God would come to pass. Mary and Martha were there when the Lord acted on their faith and raised Lazarus from the dead.

 This Mary should not be confused with Mary, the mother of Jesus, or Mary, the mother of Mark, or Mary Magdalene.

 Lazarus was dead for four days before Christ brought him back to life. This spectacular miracle inspired Jesus's enemies to finally plot to kill Him.

 The home of Mary and Martha in Bethany was the headquarters for Jesus and His closest friends during the last week of His life.

 Mary anointed Jesus during the last week of His life as a symbolic preparation for His burial.

 "She saith unto him, Yea, Lord: I believe that thou art the Christ, the Son of God, which should come into the world" (John 11:27).

Martha, Martha (Luke 10)

One day during the ministry of Jesus, He went to the city of Bethany, where Mary and Martha lived. The two sisters invited Him into their home and were honored to have Him there. Jesus sat and began to teach, as He always did. Mary, one of the sisters, sat down at His feet and listened carefully to the beautiful things that her Master was sharing. As He taught, Martha tried to listen, but she was distracted and busy, overwhelmed with getting things right for her special guest. She was cleaning, preparing food, and trying to serve Jesus and any others that came with Him. Exhausted and frustrated, she finally went to the Lord and complained about her sister, Mary. She asked Jesus to convince Mary that she should help Martha instead of sitting down and listening.

"And Jesus answered and said unto her, Martha, Martha, thou art careful and troubled about many things: But one thing is needful: and Mary hath chosen that good part." (Luke 10:41–42)

Jesus recognized Martha's hard work and knew that she was trying very hard to make everything perfect for Him, but He wanted her to know that there was something else happening that was more important. The food she was making would be good, but it would not last through eternity. The words He was sharing were better and would last forever.

There are some things in this life that are good. There are other things that are better. Some things are best of all. If we are not careful, we, like Martha, can accidentally miss the best things because we are too busy with the good things. Choosing good things is good, but don't let them keep you from the best.

? Will you choose the good, the better, and the best things in life? Will you choose the best first?

Activity

Cut up pieces of paper with movie and book titles, sports, activities we can participate in, and so on written on them. Label three jars "Good," "Better," and "Best." Take turns putting the papers in the jars where you think they belong. Have a discussion about the things that matter most.

The Four Gospels

Pharisees & Sadducees

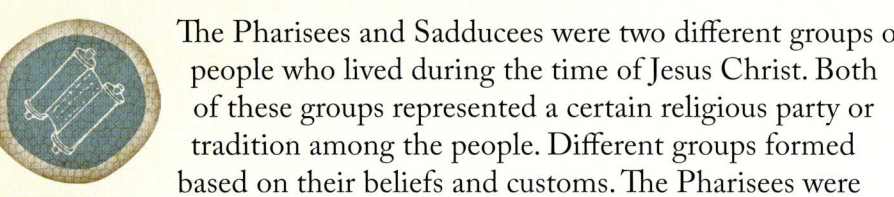 The Pharisees and Sadducees were two different groups of people who lived during the time of Jesus Christ. Both of these groups represented a certain religious party or tradition among the people. Different groups formed based on their beliefs and customs. The Pharisees were very proud of their strict obedience to the laws. They believed they were separate and better than anyone else who was a non-Israelite. To them, keeping the rules was the most important part of religion. Most of the common people agreed with the Pharisees. The Sadducees had different beliefs about the scriptures than the Pharisees, and the two groups often did not get along with each other. Generally, the Sadducees were the wealthy and the ruling priests and leaders among the people. They were in charge of the temple and everything that happened there. One of the only things these two groups agreed on was trying to stop the work of Jesus Christ.

 Members of both the Pharisees and the Sadducees made up a group of seventy-one people called the Sanhedrin. They were the highest court and made decisions on tough questions and issues that applied to all Jews.

 The Sanhedrin was led by the high priest, Caiaphas. He was influential and directed the capture, trial, and Crucifixion of Jesus Christ.

 Nicodemus was a Pharisee and member of the Sanhedrin who learned for himself that Jesus was the Christ. He defended Jesus at His trial before the Sanhedrin and helped with His burial.

 Joseph of Arimathea was another influential member of the Sanhedrin who was a follower of Jesus. Like Nicodemus, he opposed the decision to crucify Him. He provided the tomb where Jesus was buried.

 "Woe unto you, scribes and Pharisees, hypocrites! for ye are like unto whited sepulchres, which indeed appear beautiful outward, but are within full of dead men's bones, and of all uncleanness" (Matthew 23:27).

Better Than No One (Mark 3)

On a Sabbath day during His ministry, Jesus came across a man in one of the synagogues, or houses of worship, who had a withered hand. As Jesus entered in, He saw the man with the crippled hand and had compassion on him. A group of Pharisees stood off to the side, watching to see if Jesus would heal the man. They believed and taught that it was against the laws of God to heal someone on the Sabbath day, because doing so was a type of work. Jesus knew the Pharisees' hearts and asked them if it was against the law to do good on the Sabbath, but they did not answer.

"And when he had looked round about on them with anger, being grieved for the hardness of their hearts, he saith unto the man, Stretch forth thine hand." (Mark 3:5)

The man with the crippled hand stretched it out to Jesus, and Jesus made him whole. The man walked away with gladness, and the Pharisees walked away with anger. Right away they started planning a way to destroy Jesus for what He had done. They were so focused on keeping the rules that they did not see the need to help a hurting man.

Sometimes we are like the Pharisees. We focus on what is wrong in other people or think about how we might be better than them—even at church! We think we are better because we work harder, or dress nicer, or follow the commandments better. Thinking these things about ourselves distracts us from loving others. We aren't better than anyone we meet, and everyone we meet could use a little more love.

? Will you be quick to love and slow to judge? When you see others, will you wonder how you can love them instead of noticing how they might be doing things wrong?

Activity

Read the story of the good Samaritan together from Luke 10. Talk about what it means to be a true Christian to others—especially to those who are different than us.

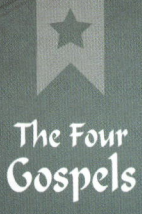

The Four Gospels
Judas Iscariot

Judas Iscariot was one of Jesus's chosen Twelve Apostles during His ministry on the earth. Judas is most well known for being the person who betrayed Jesus and turned Him over to those who wanted to kill Him. Judas was with Jesus throughout His three years of teaching, service, and miracles, but for some reason, this chosen Apostle turned against the Savior. Judas led the soldiers of the Jewish officials to the Garden of Gethsemane when he knew Jesus would be there. Judas betrayed Jesus with a kiss so the guards knew who to arrest. The Jewish officials paid him thirty pieces of silver for the betrayal. Jesus knew that Judas had planned the betrayal, but He did not stop him. Judas was the treasurer for the Twelve Apostles and handled all of the money. During that time, he had been stealing money from the money bag for himself. Judas died in shame soon after Jesus's Crucifixion and was buried in a field near Jerusalem.

 Iscariot most likely refers to his hometown, Kerioth, which was either in Moab or a place called Hazor in the south. Judas was the only one of the Twelve who was not from Galilee.

 This Judas should not be mistaken for other men in the Bible named Judas, including another disciple called "Judas the brother of James" and Judas the brother of Jesus.

 A man named Matthias replaced Judas in the Twelve Apostles after Judas died.

 Thirty pieces of silver is designated in the book of Exodus as the price of a slave.

 "But Jesus said unto [Judas], betrayest thou the Son of man with a kiss?" (Luke 22:48).

Regret and Remorse (Matthew 27)

Judas Iscariot was a good and righteous man when Jesus chose him to be one of His closest friends and disciples. No one really knows why Judas betrayed the Savior. Perhaps he was greedy for the money. Maybe he did not believe Jesus anymore. It could have been jealousy or pride. Whatever the reason was, one day Judas decided that he loved something else more than he loved the Lord. The chief priests paid Judas his money, and the plan went forward. Jesus was arrested at night and taken away. After Jesus's arrest, Judas decided he wanted to return the money and undo what he had done. But the chief priests would not take the money back.

"I have sinned in that I have betrayed the innocent blood. And they said, What is that to us? see thou to that." (Matthew 27:4)

The chief priests did not care about Judas. Judas threw the money down and ran away. He died soon after that in great sadness and regret.

We may be tempted to lie to, steal from, or mistreat other people. We may think it is worth doing because we will get something we want in exchange. However, whenever we hurt another person or God, we will eventually feel deep sadness and wish we had not done it. That is called regret. God is willing to forgive us when we repent, but that doesn't take away all the negative consequences of our choice.

? Will you remember the lesson of Judas and strive to avoid regret by choosing the right? When you make a mistake, will you think about others' feelings and quickly try to make things right?

Activity

Get a tube of toothpaste. Have someone empty the toothpaste into a bowl. Now ask him or her to put it all back in. Explain that some messes can be made really easily, and though they may seem fun, they can take a lot of work to clean up. Talk about being careful in what we do and say and always considering the consequences.

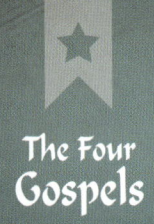

The Four Gospels

Thomas

 Thomas was one of Jesus's original Twelve Apostles. He was with the Lord throughout His travels and teachings. We do not know what Thomas's job was before he was called into the Twelve or anything about his family or earlier life. Sometimes he is referred to as "Doubting Thomas" since he did not believe the other Apostles had seen the resurrected Savior until he saw for himself. But Thomas was also very bold. At the end of Jesus' ministry, when He told His disciples it was time to go into Jerusalem, most of them were afraid and thought they would be killed. Thomas spoke up and showed his courage and willingness to die with the Lord if he must. After the Ascension of Jesus into heaven, Thomas continued to preach the good news and the Resurrection of Jesus throughout the world with the rest of the disciples.

 Thomas is also referred to throughout the Gospels by his Greek name, Didymus.

 He was given the nickname of "Doubting Thomas" when he refused to believe the other disciples about Jesus's Resurrection. He wanted to see the proof for himself.

 Thomas and the other Apostles saw the Lord in a place called the "upper room." It is believed it was in the home of the Apostle Mark's mother. It was also the place of the Last Supper.

 Historical tradition is that Thomas traveled to India as a missionary and was killed and buried there.

 "Then said Thomas, which is called Didymus, unto his fellow disciples, Let us also go, that we may die with him" (John 11:16).

Believe (John 20)

After the burial of their Master, Jesus Christ, the Twelve Apostles were very frightened, sad, and confused. They did not know what to do next or what would happen to their little group of believers. After three days of sadness, Easter Sunday came and Jesus was resurrected. Some of His closest disciples saw and talked with Him. Stories of Jesus's return started to be told among the believers. Sometime on that first Easter day, the disciples were gathered together in a place of safety. As they met together, Jesus appeared to them. He showed them the wounds in His hands, feet, and side. It was a beautiful and sacred occasion. Thomas was the only living member of the Twelve Apostles who was not there. When Thomas came later, Jesus was gone, but the others told him about their experience. Thomas told them he could not believe them unless he saw and felt the prints in His hands for himself. Eight days later, the group was gathered again in the same room. This time, Thomas was there when the Savior appeared to them. He called forth Thomas by name and invited him to feel the prints for himself. Thomas cried out in praise and in worship.

"Jesus saith unto him, Thomas, because thou hast seen me, thou hast believed: blessed are they that have not seen, and yet have believed." (John 20:29)

Each of the disciples was an eyewitness of the Resurrection of Jesus Christ. The Apostles shared their testimonies in any way they could so that others would believe in Jesus Christ. There were others who had not seen the risen Savior but still believed. We are part of those who believe in Jesus without seeing Him, too. We are followers who can read the testimony of His disciples and live and love and believe.

? Will you choose to believe in the testimonies of the Savior's witnesses that He lives?

Activity

Play Twenty Questions. After a few rounds of guessing things that you can see and touch (objects, animals, people, etc.) choose *love* as the word to be guessed for the final round. After the round, explain that even though we cannot see some things, we can still feel them and know that they are real.

The Four Gospels

Mary Magdalene

 Mary Magdalene was a faithful and devoted follower and disciple of Jesus Christ during His ministry on the earth. In addition to the Twelve Apostles, there were many other disciples who followed the teachings of Jesus. Some of these are mentioned by name, and others are not. Mary Magdalene is one of the disciples who is mentioned often and was present at very important moments in Jesus's life. She is also one of the few female disciples mentioned by name. Mary Magdalene was present at the Crucifixion of the Savior. John wrote that she stood with Mary, Jesus's mother, and Mary, the wife of Cleophas. She was also there for the Savior's burial. Mary went to the tomb on the Sunday morning after Jesus was buried. She saw the open tomb and spoke with the angels who were waiting there. She brought the news to Peter and John that Jesus was risen. Jesus appeared to Mary Magdalene, and she was the first person to ever see and speak with the resurrected Christ. She shared her witness with the rest of the disciples.

 Although we do not have many details, Jesus at one point cast seven devils out of Mary Magdalene.

 Mary Magdalene should not be confused with Mary, the mother of Jesus, or Mary, the sister of Martha.

 Magdalene is a reference to Mary's hometown of Magdala. It was a city on the coast of the Sea of Galilee.

 Mary was at the tomb alone, crying, when Jesus appeared to her. She did not recognize Him until he called her name.

 "Jesus saith unto her, Mary. She turned herself, and saith unto him, Rabboni; which is to say, Master" (John 20:16).

Bring Your Finest (John 19–20)

During the final days of Jesus's life, many of His disciples showed Him their love and devotion through the things they did. Mary, the sister of Martha, anointed Him with expensive oils the day before He rode into Jerusalem. Nicodemus defended Him before the Sanhedrin. Joseph of Arimathea went to Pilate to beg for His body so they could bury Him properly. Jesus was buried in Joseph's own family tomb. Mary Magdalene was there during Jesus's last days showing her own devotion. She stood by His mother at the foot of the cross. She helped Joseph and Nicodemus as they covered and prepared His body and put it in the tomb. Because of the laws, they could not take care of His body the way they wanted to the night He died. So they waited.

"The first day of the week cometh Mary Magdalene early, when it was yet dark, unto the sepulchre." (John 20:1)

Before the sun even started to rise on the third day, Mary was back at the tomb. She went with expensive oils and spices that she would put into His tomb as a sign of respect and love for Him. When she arrived, the tomb was empty! She ran to get the other disciples. She cried in concern for His body. She waited by the tomb, and suddenly, Jesus was there. She was privileged to be the first person to see the resurrected Lord.

Mary's love for Jesus was shown in so many ways. She showed that the Lord was worth waiting for. He was worth running for. He was worth waking up before the sun and was worth every penny of the expensive oils and perfumes she brought.

Jesus Christ is our hero, our Savior, and dearest Friend in life and death. He is worth anything we can do or say to sing praises to His name. He always deserves our very best and very finest.

 Will you always give Jesus your very best and finest?

Activity

Ask each person to write down one gift he or she wants to offer to the Savior through the coming month. Wrap a box beautifully and put it where it will remind everyone that He is worth giving our very best.

The Four Gospels

Pontius Pilate

Pontius Pilate was a Roman leader during the time of Jesus. He was the prefect, or governor, over Judea, which included the capital city of Jerusalem. Rome controlled most of the ancient world, and their emperor chose people to rule over certain areas as governors. Pilate was appointed to this position by the emperor named Tiberius, who was the leader of all Roman lands. Judea was a difficult area to rule because of the hatred the Jews had toward the Romans. Pontius Pilate was not a compassionate leader of the Jews. He did cruel things to show them his power. Pilate was involved in the trial and condemnation of Jesus. The Jews wanted to kill Jesus, but it was a Roman law that the Jewish government could not put someone to death. The chief priests sent Jesus to Pilate and said that He was trying to take over as king. Pilate eventually gave the chief priests permission to crucify Jesus. He did not serve many more years as the governor.

 Pilate served as governor of Judea for ten years.

 Herod Antipas was the governor over the Galilee area. He and Pilate sent Jesus back and forth for trials. Neither of them wanted responsibility.

 Pilate washed his hands when he turned Jesus over to the chief priests. This was a symbol that meant he was not responsible for Jesus's death.

 Pilate lived in the coastal city of Caesarea, but he would come to Jerusalem during festivals and feasts to help control the crowds.

 "When Pilate saw that he could prevail nothing, but that rather a tumult was made, he took water, and washed his hands before the multitude, saying, I am innocent of the blood of this just person: see ye to it" (Matthew 27:24).

Pilate's Pressure (Luke 23)

Pontius Pilate was in a very difficult position. Other governors before him had lost their jobs and been banished because they could not control the Jews. Pilate probably knew that the Jews would revolt and rebel if Jesus was allowed to go free. When Jesus was brought to Pilate, the governor interviewed Him and asked Him questions. Pilate soon realized that Jesus was innocent, but the crowds were pushing for permission to crucify Him. The night before the trial, Pilate's wife had a dream about Jesus. She begged Pilate to let Him go. She also knew He was innocent. Pilate sent Jesus to Herod, hoping that Herod would deal with the problem, but Herod sent Him back. It was a tradition at Passover for the governor to release one prisoner as a sign of mercy. Pilate tried to convince the crowds to have Jesus released, but they chose a thief and murderer instead. In desperation, Pilate had Jesus whipped and hoped the crowds would be satisfied with that punishment for Him. They did not give in. They yelled even louder!

"And they were instant with loud voice . . . And the voices of them and of the chief priests prevailed. And Pilate gave sentence that it should be as they required." (Luke 23:23–24)

Pilate gave in to the pressure. He sent an innocent man—Jesus—to be crucified. Pilate had the power to stop it, but he gave in to please the crowd and keep his position as the governor.

There are times when it is hard to do what is right. It is even harder when people are pressing us and trying to convince us to go against our conscience. Popularity is not a wise way to decide what is right.

? Will you stand by what is right, even when it isn't popular? Will you choose what is good even if people are pressuring you to choose what is wrong?

Activity

Set up an easy treasure hunt with a compass. Give the compass to one person to find the treasure. Give everyone else magnets that will pull the arrow off course. After a while, let them all work together. Talk about how others can either pull us off course or help us stay on course.

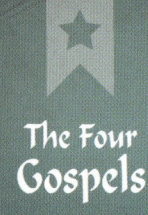

The Four Gospels

John the Apostle

 John was one of the first men called by Jesus to serve as one of the Twelve Apostles. He is often referred to as John the Beloved. He was acquainted with Peter and was a fisherman as well. His brother James was also called by the Lord to become one of the Twelve Apostles. John was with the Savior on many special occasions. He was invited to witness many of Jesus's miracles, including when He raised Jairus's daughter from the dead and when Jesus was transfigured on the Mount of Transfiguration. When Mary Magdalene found the tomb empty, she came and told John and Peter, who both ran to the tomb to see for themselves. After Jesus ascended back to heaven, John was close companions with Peter, and they faithfully taught and led the Church. For the rest of their lives, they performed miracles, suffered persecution, and visited and wrote letters to the Saints to inspire and uplift them.

 John and his brother James were given the nickname "Sons of Thunder" by Jesus at the beginning of their ministry.

 It is common belief that John was the writer of the Gospel of John, the three Epistles of John, and the book of Revelation.

 This John is not the same as John the Baptist, who baptized Jesus.

 John often refers to himself in his own Gospel as "the disciple whom Jesus loved." This does not mean Jesus did not love the others; it probably means John appreciated the love he felt from the Lord.

 "That which we have seen and heard declare we unto you, that ye also may have fellowship with us: and truly our fellowship is with the Father, and with his Son Jesus Christ. And these things write we unto you, that your joy may be full" (1 John 1:3–4).

Loyal, Loved, and Trusted (John 1–21)

During some of Jesus's darkest moments, John the Apostle was there right by His side. Hours before the Savior's betrayal and arrest, John sat right next to Him at the Last Supper. When Jesus prayed in great agony in the Garden of Gethsemane, John was waiting right outside. When Jesus was being tried and condemned in the illegal trial in Caiaphas's palace, John was there with Him. The Gospels don't include many things John said, but his presence is always recognized. He truly was a valued friend and companion to the Savior. As Jesus hung on the cross, John stood right by Him, comforting Mary. Jesus, in great compassion, said some of the last words He spoke in mortality to John:

"When Jesus therefore saw his mother, and the disciple standing by, whom he loved, he saith unto his mother, Woman, behold thy son!" (John 19:26)

John understood this simple phrase to mean that Jesus was putting the care of His beloved mother into his hands. Jesus trusted John to watch out for His mother.

John seemed to be close by the Savior at every turn in His ministry. He was loyal to the Lord from the time he was called until the very end. Jesus loved him and also trusted him.

John was not perfect, but his life was a pattern that we can strive to follow. It was a pattern that was steady and sure—a pattern of loyalty and trust. It has been said that it is great to be loved, but more valuable to be trusted.

? Can Jesus trust us in the same way He trusted John? Does He know He can count on us to be loyal and loving to the very end?

Activity

Find video clips of two types of Olympic races—a sprint and a long-distance run. Watch them and pay attention to the difference in the running. Talk about what it means to be loyal and trustworthy our entire lives.

Book of Acts

Ananias and Sapphira

Ananias and Sapphira were husband and wife Christians living in the area near Jerusalem soon after the Ascension of Jesus Christ into heaven. After the Resurrection, the Lord spent at least forty days with the disciples and members of His Church. Before He left the earth, He put His Twelve Apostles in charge of His Church and commissioned them to go to all areas of the world to teach and baptize in His name. Peter took the role as the head of the Church. During that time, members of the Church lived in a special kind of community. They agreed as part of their membership to share things with one another. If they sold property or made money, they promised to give it to the Apostles, and the Apostles would distribute it to all the members of the Church. Ananias and Sapphira were members of the Church who sold some of their property and then kept some of it back for themselves without telling anyone. As a result of their dishonesty, they both died right after they lied to the Lord and the leaders of His Church.

 We do not know when Ananias and Sapphira joined the Church or whether they knew Jesus Christ in His life.

 This story is the first time the group of followers of Jesus is referred to as a church.

 This community of Church members "had all things in common." When everyone was honest about it, no one lacked anything they needed.

 This Ananias is not the same Ananias whom Saul was sent to by the Lord after Saul's vision on the road to Damascus (see Acts 9:10–17).

 "And the multitude of them that believed were of one heart and of one soul: neither said any of them that ought of the things which he possessed was his own; but they had all things common" (Acts 4:32).

If You Lie, You Die (Acts 5)

The story of Ananias and Sapphira is so shocking! When the couple sold their property, they decided together in secret that they were going to keep part of the money and hide it from the Church. They had promised that they would share any money they made with their fellow Church members, just as the other Church members had promised to share with them. If they didn't want to live this way, they didn't have to. Instead, they wanted to benefit from everyone else without being fully committed themselves. When Ananias took a portion of the money to Peter, the great Apostle knew right away that he was lying about it being the whole amount.

> *"Why hath Satan filled thine heart to lie to the Holy Ghost, and to keep back part . . . thou hast not lied unto men but unto God."* (Acts 5:3–4)

After hearing this, Ananias immediately dropped dead to the ground.

Three hours later, his wife, Sapphira, came to see Peter. The couple had agreed and schemed earlier about the details of the lie that they would tell the Apostles when they got there. Peter gave Sapphira a chance to confess her lie and tell the truth. Instead, she stuck to the lie just as her husband had, and just like her husband, she dropped dead to the ground. The two of them were buried, and God taught a very powerful lesson to the members of the Church about sin and its consequences.

Honesty is very important to the Lord. Any time we sin and try to cover it up, there are consequences. We may not die like these two early Church members did, but part of our self-worth and good nature will die inside of us. Trying to cover our sins will never get us ahead.

 Will you strive to be completely honest in all that you do?

Activity

Drop a quarter into a bucket filled with water. Have everyone take turns dropping pennies in the bucket, trying to cover the quarter. Teach everyone that this is what lying is like. As we try to cover our lies and sins, it gets harder and harder and messier and messier.

Book of Acts

Paul (Saul)

Paul was a mighty missionary and Apostle whose life story, mission logs, and writings make up a major portion of the New Testament. Paul was born to very religious parents in the city of Tarsus. His parents named him Saul. Tarsus was a Greek city that was a part of the Roman Empire. Because of his family and birthplace, Saul spoke Greek, understood Greek and Roman culture, and was also a Roman citizen. He moved to Jerusalem during his young adult years and studied Jewish law diligently. After the Resurrection of Christ, Saul became a dedicated persecutor of the followers of Jesus. He threatened them, imprisoned them, and tried to destroy the Church. He even stood by and watched as Stephen, the first martyr of Christianity, was stoned to death. On a trip to the city of Damascus, where he intended to imprison more Christians, Saul was stopped on the road by a bright light. He heard and saw the Lord and was commanded to stop persecuting His Church. Saul made a major change and became a powerful Apostle and missionary for the Savior. From then on he was known as Paul. He traveled all over the Roman Empire teaching, testifying, and bringing souls unto Christ.

 Saul was from the tribe of Benjamin and was most likely named after King Saul. Paul was his Roman name, and he went by it on his missions. Being a Roman gave him privileges in the Roman Empire.

 Paul was a tentmaker. He used this skill to pay for his missions.

 Fourteen of the twenty-two epistles in the New Testament were written by Paul to people in the cities he had visited.

 Paul went on three major missions during his life that we know of. His missions took him thousands of miles.

 "I have fought a good fight, I have finished my course, I have kept the faith: Henceforth there is laid up for me a crown of righteousness, which the Lord, the righteous judge, shall give me at that day: and not to me only, but unto all them also that love his appearing" (2 Timothy 4:7–8).

Seek an Errand (Acts 9–28)

Saul was on his way to the city of Damascus to arrest any Christians he could find and throw them in jail. Most of the followers of Jesus knew his name and were afraid of him. As he traveled down the road, suddenly a light brighter than the sun appeared and shone all around him. Temporarily blinded, Saul heard a voice calling to him, asking him why he was persecuting the Church. When Saul asked who had spoken, the voice told him it was Jesus, whom he was fighting against. At that moment, Saul asked a question that would change his life.

"And he trembling and astonished said, Lord, what wilt thou have me to do?" (Acts 9:6)

The Savior sent Saul to a disciple named Ananias, who healed Saul's blindness, baptized him, and set him on a journey that would take him all over the Roman Empire. Saul then became Paul. He served alongside Peter, John, Luke, and other mighty Apostles and missionary companions. He testified of Jesus before governors, kings, and rulers of cities and nations. Mighty miracles happened by his word and his hand. Perhaps the best parts of these journeys were the faithful Saints he met, spent his days with, and grew to love. All these experiences started with a question that became the pattern of his life. Every day he awoke and asked the same question: "What wilt thou have me do?" Because Paul asked that question, Jesus was able to save him. Because he asked that question again and again, Jesus was able to save so many others.

We can follow this same pattern in our own lives. Imagine the great instrument we could become in the hands of the Lord if we began each day with that same question.

? Will you look to God each morning and ask Him what He would have you do? What errands does He have for you today?

Activity

Talk about what it means to run an errand for someone. Invite everyone for the next week to start each day with Paul's question. Every day, seek an errand from the Lord. Share your experiences with each other.

Philip

Book of Acts

Philip was a powerful and trusted missionary and assistant to the Twelve Apostles during the days after the Resurrection of Jesus Christ. As the Church began to grow, God commanded the Twelve to select seven men who could assist them in the work. Philip was one of the seven men chosen. He was described as a man who was honest, trustworthy, and full of the Holy Ghost. When Saul (Paul) began to persecute the Church and many of the Christians in Jerusalem scattered, Philip went to Samaria to preach the gospel there. He performed many miracles there and had wonderful success as many people began to believe in the Savior and His gospel. Later in his life, Philip had a home in Caesarea where Paul and Luke stopped to stay while they were on their third mission. Philip, often called Philip the evangelist, played an important part in the growth of the Church in its early days.

 Stephen was another one of the seven men who were chosen to assist the Twelve Apostles. He was stoned to death after refusing to stop bearing testimony of the Savior.

 Philip is the first recorded missionary to take the gospel to a city of people who were not Jews—the Samaritans.

 This is not the same Philip who was one of the original Twelve Apostles during the Savior's ministry.

 Philip had at least four daughters who had the gift to prophesy.

 "Then Philip opened his mouth, and began at the same scripture, and preached unto him Jesus" (Acts 8:35).

Run! (Acts 8)

As the Christians from Jerusalem started to spread out from the capital city, the disciples and other missionaries began to travel to more distant places. Philip chose Samaria as one of the first places he would labor. Many Jews did not even want to walk through Samaria, but Philip knew that Jesus's love for people was not determined by where they were from. Philip performed miracles and taught the people of that city with great power and influence. Word of Philip's great success spread all the way to Jerusalem. In the middle of all of the excitement and missionary efforts, an angel spoke to Philip and commanded him to go to the remote and lonely desert south of Jerusalem. Philip went right away. When he arrived, he saw an Ethiopian man of authority riding in a carriage.

> *"Then the Spirit said unto Philip, Go near, and join thyself to this chariot. And Philip ran."* (Acts 8:29–30)

When Philip got to the chariot, he found the man inside was reading from Isaiah and having trouble understanding it. Philip taught him from the scriptures about Jesus and His message of love. The Ethiopian was so moved, he stopped the chariot by a lake and asked Philip to baptize him.

When Philip heard the voice of the angel instruct him to leave his success in Samaria and head to a desert place, he went immediately. When he saw a stranger from a distant land passing in a chariot, the Spirit said go, and Philip ran. He ran! He was known for not only his obedience, but for quick obedience. The Lord knew that if He needed something done—even quickly—He could ask Philip. What about you?

? When the Lord asks you to do something, will you run to get it done? Will you obey quickly?

Activity

Throw coins, buttons, or cards all over the floor in a room. Time someone picking them all up. Throw them out again and challenge the person to beat his or her time. Perhaps people can try to beat each other's times for extra fun. Talk about doing the Lord's work quickly and with enthusiasm.

King Agrippa II

Book of Acts

King Agrippa was a member of the Herod family and was the last ruler of that family dynasty in the Roman Empire. The Herods ruled over areas where Jesus and His disciples lived and ministered, and they were often an important part of their stories. The Herods were generally terrible, wicked, and awful rulers. When Rome began to take control over the area where the Jews (Israelites) were living, Herod the Great, a friend of Caesar Augustus, was put in control of the entire region. When that Herod died, the area was divided among his three sons, Herod Archelaus, Herod Philip, and Herod Antipas. After the reign of these three men, a new Caesar put Herod Agrippa in charge of the whole area and gave him the title of king. He was a selfish leader and very cruel to the Christians. At his death, his son, Agrippa II, was only seventeen years old. After six years, Caesar gave a smaller area to Agrippa II and allowed him to keep the title of king. The Apostle Paul was able to share his conversion story and testimony of Christ with Agrippa II during a trial. When Agrippa II died, the Herodian dynasty ended.

 Herod the Great was Agrippa II's great-grandfather. Herod the Great is the king who was visited by the wise men and who ordered all the babies to die in Bethlehem when Jesus was born.

 Agrippa II was the king when the Romans destroyed Jerusalem in AD 70.

 Herod Agrippa I, Agrippa II's father, had a sister-in-law named Herodias. She was the wicked woman who convinced her husband, Herod Antipas, to kill John the Baptist.

 Herod Agrippa I was the king who killed James the Apostle and tried to kill Peter. He died from a disease he caught on the day he paraded around as a god.

 "King Agrippa, believest thou the prophets? I know that thou believest" (Acts 26:27).

Almost and Altogether (Acts 26)

During Paul's third mission, he spent some of his time back in Jerusalem. While he was there, a large group of people became angry with him and wanted to kill him. His nephew knew of their secret plans and warned Paul. Because Paul was a Roman citizen, the Roman soldiers took him to the city of Caesarea to keep him safe. He stayed there for two years under house arrest. While he was there, he had an opportunity to tell his story and teach the governors of that city. When King Agrippa II came to Caesarea to visit, the governor, Festus, took Paul in to see the king so he could hear Paul's story. Paul told the king about his life persecuting the Christians. He told him about his journey to Damascus when the Savior stopped him in a bright light. He told the king of his conversion. Paul then bore his powerful witness of the living and resurrected Jesus Christ. King Agrippa II listened carefully to the story of Paul, and he felt something in his heart.

"Then Agrippa said unto Paul, Almost thou persuadest me to be a Christian. And Paul said, I would to God, that not only thou, but also all . . . were both almost, and altogether such as I am." (Acts 26:28–29)

The king then told the governor that Paul was innocent of all the charges that were keeping him in Caesarea. Unfortunately, the king also continued to live the rest of his life as "almost" a Christian.

We can either live like King Agrippa II and "almost" decide to be a follower of Jesus Christ, or we can be like Paul and be a Christian altogether. We can choose to be 100 percent Christian 100 percent of the time.

? Will you be almost or altogether a believer and follower of Jesus Christ?

Activity

Bake a cake together and put it in the oven at almost the right temperature and cook it for almost the right amount of time. Take it out and serve it—mushy and uncooked. Talk about the difference between almost and altogether. (Make sure you have a backup dessert!)

Book of Acts

Lydia, the Seller of Purple

During Paul's missionary journeys, he met all sorts of people. Some of them were wicked, some of them were strange, and some of them became faithful believers of Jesus Christ. Lydia was one of the faithful women that Paul met and baptized during his ministry. During Paul's second missionary journey, he felt uneasy about going to two of the cities he was planning to visit. One night, he had a dream that directed him to go to a certain part of Europe where there were many non-believers. He arrived in a city called Philippi, and on the Sabbath he went to a riverside, where he heard people gathered to pray. There, he met Lydia and other faithful women. Lydia owned a business and was successful selling purple clothing and other textiles. She believed in Paul's message before he ever spoke to her. Lydia and her whole household were baptized. She pleaded with Paul and his companions to stay at her home so that she could take care of them while they were in her city. Paul stayed there for many days before journeying on.

 Lydia was from an area called Thyatira, which was well known for producing a purple dye that couldn't be found other places.

 Paul wrote his epistle to the Philippians for the Saints in Lydia's city.

 Lydia is considered the first recorded convert in Europe.

 Paul was put in prison while staying in Philippi. In jail, he taught and baptized the jailor, who became one of the many Christians who gathered for church at Lydia's home.

 "And a certain woman named Lydia, a seller of purple, of the city of Thyatira, which worshipped God, heard us: whose heart the Lord opened" (Acts 16:14).

Purple Hands (Acts 16)

Paul described Lydia in his missionary journals as "a seller of purple." She was well known in her area for selling purple clothing. Perhaps she wore purple herself. If she was involved in the dying of the clothes, she would have had purple hands from her work. The people in her city, and even strangers, would have been able to quickly recognize the signs that she was a seller of purple.

Lydia knew something about God and His gospel before she ever met Paul. When the Apostle came to her city, she already had the habit of gathering with other faithful women near the river to pray. The Lord opened her heart to accept Paul's message. Immediately after her baptism, she begged Paul to allow her to host him, Silas, and Timothy at her home while they taught the people of the area.

"If ye have judged me to be faithful to the Lord, come into my house, and abide there. And she constrained us." (Acts 16:15)

Paul agreed. He could immediately tell that Lydia was a faithful believer in Jesus Christ. Her faith in the Savior was obvious—just as her business was obvious to other people, too.

What we do on the outside is often a reflection of what is happening in our hearts. Our faith in Jesus Christ should be easy to recognize. It should be obvious when people meet us, see the way that we act, and hear the things we say. If someone came to our room or home, they should be able to recognize our faith quickly. It should leave a mark or an impression on them. It should be as obvious as if we had purple hands.

? When people meet you, will they know of your love for and belief in Jesus Christ? Will your words and actions give you away?

Activity

Color one of your fingers purple by dipping it in dye or coloring on it with a nontoxic marker. As you go to work and school, people will ask you what it means. Tell them the story of faithful Lydia, or simply tell them it is a family sign that you are a believer in Jesus Christ.

Jesus Christ

The Holy Bible

Ever since the time of Adam and Eve, the people of God looked forward to the coming of their Savior, Jesus Christ. All the prophets, priests, and poets in the Old Testament spent their lives teaching about His coming to the world. Jesus was born to Mary in the city of Bethlehem in a stable for animals. He grew up in the city of Nazareth, near the Sea of Galilee. Around the age of thirty, He began His public ministry by being baptized by John the Baptist. He called Twelve Apostles, established His church, and spent His days ministering to the poor and needy. He taught people in parables and performed mighty miracles in the areas around Galilee, Samaria, and Jerusalem. Jesus was betrayed by one of His closest disciples and was crucified by His enemies. His body was placed in a borrowed tomb, but He rose again in triumphant Resurrection—the first person to ever do such a thing. He left His disciples with instructions to continue His work in every nation even after He ascended to heaven.

 Jesus has many titles. One of the most frequently used is *Messiah*, which means "the anointed." It is an Aramaic word (the language Jesus spoke on Earth). The Greek word for it is *Christ*.

 Many of the Jews were expecting the Savior to come and conquer the Romans for them. When He came instead teaching love and offering eternal salvation, many did not recognize Him as the prophesied Savior.

 The high priest who organized the arrest and Crucifixion of Jesus was the man who should have represented Jesus and led people to Him.

 The name Jesus is the Greek version of the Hebrew name Joshua. It means "God is help."

 "For unto us a child is born, unto us a son is given: and the government shall be upon His shoulder: and his name shall be called Wonderful, Counsellor, The mighty God, The everlasting Father, The Prince of Peace" (Isaiah 9:6).

Do Good (The Bible)

Every moment of the life of Jesus was a beautiful one. His character and goodness and mercy are as great and as wonderful as people hope they are. Every day, from before the sun came up until after the sun went down, Jesus "went about doing good" (Acts 10:38). He looked for the lonely. He sought out the people who were sad. He loved the unlovable. He showed us the way. And even after so much giving, He still had one more gift to offer. It was the gift He was born to offer. Jesus came into the world to lay down His life for His friends—to pay the ransom price for our freedom. He suffered in Gethsemane and on Calvary's cross to rescue us from sin and death. After Jesus' body lay in the tomb for three days, the disciples returned and found the tomb empty. Empty! Because He rose from the grave, the world can have a second chance. We can feel the hope and light and love that came on that first Easter Sunday. Because of Jesus Christ, we can be forgiven like Jonah, be delivered like Moses, and see miracles like Elijah. We can anticipate blessings like Elizabeth, become something more like Peter, and find healing like the leper. Jesus Christ is the God of the Old Testament, the New Testament, and our God today. When He ascended into heaven, the Twelve Apostles looked up as He went, perhaps wishing for His return. Two angels appeared unto them.

"Ye men of Galilee, why stand ye gazing up into heaven? this same Jesus, which is taken up from you into heaven, shall so come in like manner as ye have seen him go into heaven." (Acts 1:11)

The same question can be asked of us. Why are you standing here? He will come again. Yes, He will definitely come again. In the meantime, go do good, as He would do.

? Will you live your life looking to Him, loving Him, and living like Him?

Activity

Have everyone find a song, poem, painting, or anything else they like to share about Jesus. You can choose something created by someone else or take time to create your own piece. Share with each other why you love the Savior.

Meet the Author and Illustrator

By day **David Butler** is a religious educator for high school and has taught many students his love for the scriptures and the power for good innate in every human soul. By night he is a fort builder, waffle maker, sports coach and story teller for his six favorite little people. Somewhere in between those he is a motivational speaker and writer. Some of his writings can be found on a blog he co-authors—multiplygoodness.com. His darling wife Jenny and their six kids live in the snowy cities of the Mountain West but dream of a beach house on a sunny shore somewhere.

Ryan Jeppesen cultivated his love for art while growing up on a dairy farm in Northern Utah. Ryan graduated from Utah State University with a BA in Marketing and a Masters of Business Administration Degree. He spends his days working at a cushy desk job and comes home at night to fully unleash his creativity by painting, drawing, illustrating, building websites, wood carving, toy building, sculpting, bread baking, and helping with countless church projects. He and his amazing wife Brooke are raising their four "Jeppesenite" children in the snowy cities of the Mountain West . . . and they like it there.